Navigating The Real Estate World

By Merillee Booren

For every client over the years who has trusted me to help them with
such an important decisions for them
and their families, I hope I never take that for granted.
Thank you for always helping me
learn and grow from our experiences.

For my family and friends who support me in all of my endeavors, I
am forever grateful for you.

www.NavigatingRealEstateBook.com

© 2018 Merillee Booren

All rights reserved. This book or parts thereof may not be reproduced in any form, stored in any retrieval system, or transmitted in any form by any means—electronic, mechanical, photocopy, recording, or otherwise—without prior written permission of the publisher, except as provided by United States of America copyright law. For permission requests, write to the publisher at Attention: Permissions Coordinator, at the address below.

Publisher@NavigatingRealEstateBook.com

The contents provided herein are simply for educational purposes and do not take the place of legal advice. Every effort has been made to ensure that the content provided is accurate and helpful for our readers at publishing time. However, this is not an exhaustive treatment of the subjects. No liability is assumed for losses or damages due to the information provided. You are responsible for your own choices, actions, and results. You should consult professionals in your area to meet your needs including tax professionals, lenders, attorneys, and real estate brokers.

Table of Contents

Introduction 1

Building Personal Wealth Through Real Estate 3

Home Buyer's Guide 19

Chapter 1_Preparing for Homeownership 21

Building Credit 21

Affording a Home 25

Using a Buyer's Agent 28

Learning Your Market 35

Lending 38

Other terms you may hear associated with home loans . 39

Stable Pre-Approval 44

Chapter 2_Finding the Right Home 46

Writing an Offer 51

Chapter 3_The Escrow Process 57

Week One 59

Week 2 62

Week 3 63

Week 4 63

Closing 64

Chapter 4_Repeat Buyers 66

Market Conditions and Timing 69

Condition 73

Quick Buyer Review 76

Quick Seller Review 77

Are You Ready to Be a Real Estate Investor? 80

Investing in Real Estate 83

    Chapter 5 Types of Investments 85

        Cap Rate and Gross Rent Multiplier 90

        Tenant Screening 97

    Chapter 6 Managing Rental Properties 102

    Chapter 7 Financially Distressed Properties 109

        Flipping 119

Home Seller's Guide 125

    Chapter 8 Preparing to Sell 127

        What To Expect 128

    Chapter 9 Pricing, Marketing and Staging your Home 137

        Pricing Your Home 137

        Marketing Your Home- 147

        Preparing Your Home 152

        Real Estate Seasons 155

    Chapter 10 The Selling Process 157

        The Offer 157

        The Closing Process 162

        Understanding The Process 171

    Chapter 11 For Sale By Owner 172

    Chapter 12 Financially Distressed Properties 190

Conclusion 195

Introduction

Building Personal Wealth Through Real Estate

Some people think real estate is complicated, too complicated for them to really understand. There certainly are a lot of rules and regulations in place that can make it seem overwhelming, but the concept behind it is simple. The wealthy own assets. The less wealthy lease assets

In fact, it is so easy that any child old enough to play a board game can understand it. Pass GO, collect $200 and start buying real estate, as much as you can land on. If you want your property to make money for you, build something on it. If you want it to make more money for you, build something bigger on it. We've all played the game and I promise you've never won without any property cards in your hand.

Think of the wealthiest people you know. If you don't know someone personally, think of someone well known for their wealth. They may have gained wealth or notoriety in a variety of ways. Maybe they were a computer genius, maybe a publishing tycoon, or a social media magnet, but from that original source of income, they have likely expanded their personal wealth in a variety of ways. Without even knowing who you have in mind, the one thing I can guarantee they will have in common is that they own real estate, probably multiple properties in multiple markets.

Maybe Bill Gates was on your list of wealthy people. In 2015, Business Insider looked at Gates real estate holdings. "With a net worth that's estimated to be as much as $80.1 billion, Microsoft cofounder Bill Gates is the richest man in the world. Gates has exactly the kind of real estate portfolio you would expect from a billionaire, from a Washington mansion worth $123 million to multiple horse ranches across the US. Gates has also made several secretive purchases through his ultra-private investment firm, Cascade."

Media magnet Oprah Winfrey has been in the news in recent years for selling some of her many holdings in the Chicago area, diversifying to other areas of the country. She is known to own homes in New Jersey, Chicago, Florida, Colorado, Maui, and Antigua. That does not include real estate holdings in other names that ultimately tie to her personal wealth.

Real estate is the key to personal wealth. To oversimplify, it is the way you win the game. Andrew Carnegie was quoted as saying that, "90% of all millionaires become so through owning real estate. More money has been made in real estate than in all industrial investments combined."

Is being mega-wealthy necessary for having success in real estate? Franklin D. Roosevelt said, "Real estate cannot be lost or stolen, nor can it be carried away. Purchased with common sense… and managed with reasonable care, it is about the safest investment in the world."

One of my favorite aspects of building personal wealth through real estate is that it does not take millions to make it work for you. It is unique in its ability to leverage the potential asset. Have you ever heard of someone going to a bank to get a loan to buy stocks? How about for gold or other metal? Probably not. But getting a loan to buy a home is normal, and with today's low interest rates, highly attractive. Personal homes can be bought for 0% down, in some cases. Even investment properties can be purchased with 20% down. This allows you to decide how best to make your money work for you to amplify the appreciation of your asset.

Eric S. Belsky, Director of the Joint Center of Housing Studies at Harvard University stated, "Even a hefty 20% down payment results in a leverage factor of five, so that every percentage point rise in the value of the home is a 5% return on their equity. With many buyers putting 10% or less down, their leverage factor is 10 or more."

An investment in real estate does something that stocks and bonds simply cannot. It fulfills the basic human need for shelter. First and foremost when purchasing a home, it is shelter. Whether we own our shelter, or rent someone else's, we all require it; and unless we are living rent free in your mother's basement, it costs money. Let's look at an example:

Jane rents a home for 30 years, without any rental increases. (Okay, I admit, this is less an example and more a fairy tale. I have never know rental rates to stay the same for 30 years but for the sake of making the math easy for everyone…) Jane pays $1,500 a month, every month for 30 years. After 30 years, Jane has paid $540,000 for her shelter. But what does she have to show for it? What has she gained, beyond the roof over her head? Her $540,000 has provided her with 0% equity, zero benefit beyond the simple need for shelter.

Whether owning or renting, you are likely making a mortgage payment. The only question is, whose mortgage is it? And who is gaining the equity from your payment? They say in investing, where there is little to no risk, there is little to no reward, but not owning real estate may be the biggest risk of all. Let's look at Jane again:

Jane makes a modest investment of $7,000 into a $200,000 home. Her mortgage payment is $1,500 a month, which she pays every month for 30 years. After

30 years, she has payed $547,000 towards her home, which she now owns free and clear. Since her purchase 30 years before, her home has appreciated in value, on an average of 5% annually. Her home is now valued at $864,388. Not only would this mean that in reality, Jane has lived rent free for 30 years, she has also gained $317,388 that she did not have before.

Can that number be right? $864,388 for the same house, 30 years later? It certainly could. According to the 2010 Census, between 1968 and 2009, homes, nationwide, appreciated at an average of 5.4% annually. That average lets us ignore the volatility of short term gains, such as 14% in 1979, or losses, like the 15% drop in 2009 . Short term appreciation can be volatile, but long term rates show the market average over a relatively long period of time. It would seem that Jane's $7,000 initial investment worked well for her in increasing her overall wealth. I know that given the choice of the two, I would rather be the Jane from the second scenario heading into retirement. While I can never guarantee that a real estate investment will make money, I can say that historically the odds are certainly in your favor. And I can guarantee that, unlike renting, you, at the very least, have a chance.

The same Census report shows another major benefit to real estate investments, which is to use them to hedge your investments against inflation, or in other words, to make inflation work for you, rather than against you. A wealthy real estate investor I work with once told me that the only people who dislike inflation are the ones who don't have anything to inflate. Especially in the case of hyperinflation when your cash is rapidly losing value, your real estate assets value would likely be skyrocketing; all while the cost of ownership remains relatively fixed. With a fixed rate mortgage the amount owed is constant with the only variables in monthly payment being property taxes and insurance. While the rental market rates would rise with the rate of inflation, or even more so, causing your living expenses to increase over time, a fixed rate mortgage allows buyers a sense of security, locking in a fixed living expense that is immune to the chaos that inflation can cause. Belsky of Harvard stated that "housing costs and rents have tended over most time periods to go up at or higher than the rate of inflation, making owning an attractive proposition." The rate of inflation for the time period of 1968-2009 was 4.5%, meaning that real estate appreciated at a higher rate than inflation as a whole. While homeownership can protect the owner from skyrocketing living expenses, it also has the added benefit of working for the owner in gaining equity over the rate of inflation, thus building true wealth.

Beyond securing your own financial security, real estate has the ability to transfer this wealth, relatively tax sheltered, to future generations, thus giving your children a meaningful advantage in life. For many in my generation we find ourselves looking at homes and wondering if we will ever be able to afford the kind of home we grew up in. Imagine what it will be like for our children as homes continue to appreciate. Will they be able to afford Jane's now $864,000 home? Now imagine what it would be like if they inherited a property. Housing typically accounts for 1/3 of our living expenses. With 1/3 of their income returned to them, they could pay for college or invest themselves. Passing on the asset of real estate can even be leveraged in regards to inheritance taxes to limit your beneficiary's tax liability. They say that the only sure things are death and taxes. We can't avoid the first, but real estate investments do help mitigate the latter for your loved ones.

Of all these benefits, the best element of real estate as a form of wealth building over other forms of investments may be the asymmetric risk and reward. The government subsidizes home ownership with a series of tax deductions, most notably the deduction for mortgage interest. In the first year of owning a $200,000 home with 20% down, even at the low interest rate of 3.75%, the mortgage interest paid would be $7,437; the second year would be $7,297; the third would be $7,151, the fourth $7,000 and the fifth $6,843. Over 5 years, the shelter over your head, the shelter you would have to pay for regardless, would provide you with a tax deduction of $35,728. Virtually no other investment on the market can compete with that kind of government subsidy.

There is also protection for the equity gained in home ownership. Large tax exemptions keep most homeowners from owing any taxes on the proceeds from the sale of their home, even for inherited homes, given that the owner has lived in the home for two years prior to the sale. Currently the tax exemption for a single person is $250,000 or $500,000 for a married couple filing jointly. Considering the average time for first time home buyer to remain in their home is 5 years, they would likely never pay any taxes on the proceeds of their sale, creating wealth without the liability of capital gains taxation, something that is unheard of in other potential investments.

Unlike many other forms of investments, the government has put strict safeguards in place to protect property owners against practices such as predatory lending and other issues that could be harmful to homeowners. With the housing collapse of the mid-2000's, the federal government offered loan forgiveness and forbearance to struggling homeowners, even offering loan modifications to help borrowers stay in their homes. The government did this for many reasons, not the least of which is to promote local stability and maintain tax revenue for local governments. But the outcome for owners was to stabilize an investment market to save assets at risk. There are virtually no other investment opportunities that ensure such favorable protections under the law.

When all is taken into account, there's no one sure investment that is guaranteed to grow your financial wealth, but in both the long and short term, real estate has a proven track record of success. The long term financial security of stabilizing your living expenses during times of inflation bring financial security while your real estate asset appreciates in value. In the short term the volatility of the market brings more risk, but along with it, the potential of more reward. In a quickly appreciating market the benefits of a short term ownership may be too enticing for some to pass up. This reached its peak in 2005 with the advent of "flipping", owning a home for a short time, weeks or days even, possibly doing minor repairs or renovations and turning around and selling the property for a profit. Personally, I blame home improvement reality TV. No matter how easy it looks on TV, most financial analysts would advise against the extremes of this investment technique, but that didn't stop some people from turning off their TV and heading out to find a home to flip. For what it's worth, I watch medical shows on TV. That doesn't mean that I'm going to try to perform a heart surgery. I will admit that there is a great potential for those who flip properties well, but you must be willing to lose to play the game properly. Where there is great risk, there can be great reward. Your tolerance for risk is a personal matter. Even for those with a lower risk threshold, there is the possibility that even owning a home for one to five years could net a large enough equity gain to comfortably move you on to a new larger investment or give you the flexibility to sell and move at the time of your choosing.

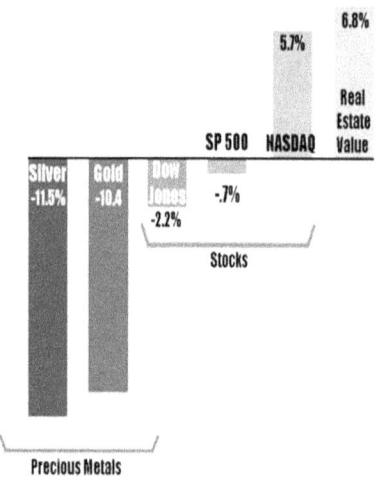

In 2015, real estate outperformed nearly all other major investment indexes. Standard savings and bank rates lingered in the .5% to 3% range, while silver dropped by 11.5% and gold was down 10.4% over the previous year. The Dow Jones was down 2.2% overall, the S&P 500 was down .7%. The NASDAQ was up 5.7%, but real estate nationwide rose 6.8% over the previous year. It was a solid year to choose real estate over other investments.

In recent years we have seen that isn't always the case. Between 2006 and 2011 we saw a national average equity loss of 30% during the housing meltdown. Some predicted that it was the death knell of homeownership in America, but that has proven to not be the case. Markets are stabilizing. Many are returning strong equity gains. Many homeowners are seeing their home values beginning to rebound to pre- meltdown levels. But even in the midst of the meltdown, the worst downturn the modern housing market has ever seen, there was never an actual loss for the homeowner who stayed the course. The losses that were recorded only existed hypothetically. No money was actually lost until a property was sold. So those who hung on through the storm, many of whom refinanced to a lower interest rate, came out as well or even ahead of where they began. Warren Buffet said "If held for a long period of time and purchased at low rates, houses are even better than stocks."

First and foremost, a house is shelter. And for all the financial benefits, there are just as many social benefits which are sometimes harder to quantify that come as part of that basic human need for shelter.

Homeownership carries benefits for both the homeowner and their family and the community in which they dwell. Homeownership and stability go hand in hand. Homeowners move far less frequently than renters. From 2010-2011 homeowners moved 4.7% of the time. Renters moved 26% of the time. (Current Population Survey,

2008-2011). This residential stability serves to strengthen social ties within a neighborhood. In 1997 researchers concluded that "social cohesion and strong ties are paths through which resources for social control are made.

As a result of these social controls, it has been shown that homeowners are far less likely to become crime victims. It also showed lower rates of domestic violence and lower rates of homicide.

Homeowners have a vested interest in protecting their neighborhoods. They are more likely to participate in local elections, to volunteer in their communities, and attend church regularly over their renting counterparts.

The phrase "pride of ownership" takes on a more literal meaning with studies showing that homeowners report a higher level of life satisfaction, self-esteem, and higher perceived control over their lives verses renters. It also showed better overall health, specifically in areas of mental health and happiness.

Still the most telling effect of homeownership may not be for the homeowner at all, but for their children. Children of homeowners perform better in school. Changes in schools caused by frequent relocations negatively affect children's educational outcomes. Regardless of income levels, children of homeowners have higher high school graduation rates, even for children living 150% below the poverty line.

The same study showed that, specifically children living 150% below the poverty line, whose parents owned a home, these children showed an increased rise in academic achievement, earnings, and independence in young adulthood "at even greater rates than children of homeowners living at more than 150% above the poverty line." These findings would suggest that the effect of homeownership on children is not due to unobserved characteristics of the homeowner themselves, but that there is a causal link between the two.

The rate of teenage pregnancy is lower among children of homeowners. These children have higher levels of achievement in math and reading and fewer behavioral problems. Research has also confirmed that access to economic and educational opportunities are more prevalent in neighborhoods with higher rates of homeownership and community involvement, giving a child the best opportunity for success in their future.

There is something about a home that lends a sense of stability and calm to a person and family. These studies show what we have probably already known to be true. We can be our best selves when we feel safe and stable. A stable home provides a sense of that for children as well as adults. As children grow in that environment, they conform to the social construct that surrounds them, encouraging more involvement in community and service to others.

With these benefits to our society as a whole, we can more easily see why the government continues to encourage homeownership in America. It is more than a financial institution. It has become part of our national makeup. It is the first step along a path of financial wellbeing and personal wealth building that is part of the quintessential American dream.

This book is meant for you, whether you are a first time buyer, a repeat buyer, a seller or an investor. The format is designed to help you find the information you are looking for quickly. It can lead you through the process to build your own wealth.

Home Buyer's Guide

Chapter 1

Preparing for Homeownership

Building Credit

Preparing for homeownership early will make the process easier for you. It takes discipline to make good credit decisions early in life. The first step is to open a bank account. It doesn't have to be a fancy account, but watch for hidden fees. If you are paid through Direct Deposit, most banks will waive the monthly fee. Others will waive the fee if you set up a checking and savings account and arrange a transfer from your checking into your savings account at least once a month. Make smart banking decisions. Find a bank that will not cost you unreasonable amounts of money to use their services. Consider local credit unions as well. Some are very competitive and they tend to have more flexible standards.

Some people hesitate to take out a credit card for fear of racking up debt, but to build credit you must use credit, and use it responsibly. The easiest credit to start with is typically gas cards or store credit cards. Being approved for a card does not mean you should go on a massive spending spree. Use these credit cards in place of your debit card, and then make sure to save the money to pay them off each month. This is the process of building credit. Once your credit has matured, you will be able to get other credit cards, car loans and other types of revolving credit. The important part is to not accumulate excessive debt, and to make your payments on time.

As your credit matures, you will want to keep an eye on things that could negatively impact your credit. Identity theft is rampant and can cause long term damage to your credit score, but so can small errors in credit reporting.

When my husband and I applied for our first home loan, we were given a copy of our credit reports and were shocked to see a revolving line of credit for a jewelry store on his report. He had bought my engagement ring five years earlier on a store credit card, which offered him 0% interest for six months. This allowed him to make three payments of $650 over the first three months, and pay the ring off without accruing any interest. Five years later it was still showing up on his credit as an active account where he owed payments of $650 a month. This made a huge difference in the home we could buy. Once the error was corrected, our purchase power increased. Careful monitoring can avoid those types of errors. There are many services that provide you with your credit score and history, even monitoring, for a fee.

AnnualCreditReport.com is an actual free site that allows you to pull all three major credit bureau reports once a year. The Federal government requires that you have annual access to your credit report free of charge. Use it to your advantage.

If there are flaws in your credit, late payments or collections, work with the debt holder to get them corrected as soon as possible. Your credit score is vital to your financial stability. Protect it.

Making payments on time has never been easier. Most large financial institutions offer services to have payments automatically withdrawn from your bank account to make sure they are paid on time. Some will even provide a discount in your payment or interest rate for signing up for these services.

If you have flexible pay days, or are a control enthusiast, such as myself, you may prefer to set up payments yourselves. Online banking is very secure and offered for free with most banks and credit unions. You can easily set up revolving payments on a specific day each month, or even go in once a month and tell the computer when to pay each bill. Most banks offer a very secure mobile banking option. Paying bills on time is as easy as opening an app and pressing a few buttons. However you choose to pay your bills, you must stay on top of them, and avoid unnecessary late payments. With these tools, started at a young age, when the time comes to think about home ownership you will be ready to take the next step.

Affording a Home

The idea of owning your own home can be exciting, but it is important to understand what you can comfortably afford so the idea of home ownership doesn't become a nightmare. Saving for a down payment is always wise. It doesn't have to be big. There are 0% down loans available in some areas and 3% to 3.5% down loans are common, especially for first time buyers. Make automatic transfers to your savings account with each deposit. It doesn't have to be a large amount. Those deposits will add up and help you reach your goal. If you are looking at $200,000 houses, you will need between $7000 and $10,000 to be able to purchase a home on an FHA program. If you qualify for a 0% down loan, it could cost as little as $1500 to purchase. While these low down payment loans will usually require mortgage insurance, if the market is appreciating, it would likely be better to purchase now and pay the insurance fees rather than waiting to save up 20%.

In addition to down payments, it is important to understand what you can afford to pay each month, and how the banks calculate how much money you will be approved for.

because he just isn't sure if he's going to be able to do it. He's hoping some time on the internet can help him figure it out himself.

He has a car payment of $215 a month, three student loan payments of $98, $113, and $240, and a credit card with a balance of about $2500, which the minimum payment is $100 a month. To find Tom's back end ratio we take his annual salary and divide it by 12 months of the year, bringing his gross monthly income to $5416. We now add all of Tom's monthly obligations, together totaling $766 a month. We only need one more figure; Tom's housing expense. Tom has looked at homes in his area and thinks he would be very happy in a $200,000 home, but he doesn't know if he can afford it. This is what we are trying to find out.

So, let's help Tom out. There are many mortgage calculators found online. Whatsmypayment.com happens to be one of my favorites, because they have very accurate calculations for mortgage insurances for different loan programs. Make sure to select the type of loan that interests you and the payment should be fairly accurate. Tom has some money to put down, but not a lot, so is looking at an FHA loan with a 3.5% down payment option. He will need one more piece of information, and that is a current interest rate for his mortgage. These rates are fluctuating all the time, but a quick online search should provide you with a rough estimate. For our purposes, we will use an interest rate of 4.25%, making his monthly payment approximately $1102 a month. So what is Tom's back end ratio? Including a house payment of $1102 and his other monthly debts of $766, Tom's monthly debt obligation is $1868 a month. $1868 divided by $5416, his gross monthly salary, means that Tom's back end ratio would be 34.5%. Assuming he has a decent credit score, he would be able to qualify for a home loan on the homes he has been looking at. Tom is ready to take the next step; as soon as he figures out what that is.

Using a Buyer's Agent

Sure, Tom could start searching homes online. There is no shortage of real estate websites, and this is how 9 in 10 homebuyers begin their search according to studies by the National Association of Realtors (National Association of Realtors, 2015). The problem is that he is missing vital pieces of information. What is the current market like in his area? How long are homes staying on the market? Are prices rising or falling? What about interest rates? A steep rise in interest rates could have a profound effect on what Tom can afford. What about sellers paying for, or at least contributing to, some of the costs associated with the purchase? Is that something that is common in Tom's market at the time? It's time for Tom to talk to a real person, or more likely, a few of them.

Some buyers want to avoid this step. I think it's because, as a profession, we real estate brokers do a rather poor job of explaining what we do and how we do it. Instead buyers wander from house to house, talking with the seller's real estate broker, who has a financial obligation to their client, not you. It's exhausting work, and often discouraging when you find a home you want to see only to be told that someone else has beaten you to it, again and again. Some buyers get discouraged and simply give up.

It is as if there is a cloud of mystery about what I do for a living; far more than there should be. When I talk to first time buyers, the question they all want to know, and no one wants to ask, is how I get paid. No one wants to talk to a professional without knowing if they will end up owing that person a lot of money for services, money that they may not be able to afford. It's a fair question. You shouldn't be afraid to ask it, especially because the answer is so simple. As a buyer's agent, I am paid by the seller. 99% of my clients owe me nothing for my services.

How this is possible? When someone decides to sell their house, they likely contact a real estate broker to list the home for sale. They sign a contract with that broker that says when Broker X sells their home they will pay him a certain percentage of the sales price, called a commission. Broker X then turns around and advertises that home for sale. One way they do that is through a website exclusive to other real estate professionals, called the MLS, or multiple listing service. In that listing, Broker X offers to pay Broker Y a certain amount of his commission, usually roughly half, for providing a ready willing and able buyer. When the transaction closes and the buyer gets keys to their new home, the brokers are paid according to those contracts. It's that simple. So you can hop from listing agent to listing agent, with no one looking out for your interests. You can put in a lot of time and energy and still be late to the party most of the time. Or you can get expert advice, instant real estate market updates, and someone making sure your needs are met, usually for free. You just can't beat free. So, why would anyone not want a buyer's agent?

Well, I did say 99% of the time. Let's look at the other 1%. There are homes on the market that are not on the MLS, usually referred to as for sale by owner homes. You can find them on many real estate websites. These are sellers who want to avoid paying a commission to real estate agents. Some want to save the money. Some have had a bad experience and hate all real estate brokers. Whatever the reason, they have chosen to go it alone. I always ask my clients to contact me first if a "for sale by owner" home interests them. Most of the time, if I call them first and ask to show the home, the seller will let me, and usually we can work out a commission paid for my services. It doesn't always work out, but usually it all comes together.

Occasionally someone will say no, they don't want to work with real estate brokers. At that point, I will step back, contact my client and explain the situation. There is nothing I want more than for you to find your home. So, if this is your house, you then have two options; you may pay me yourself, usually around 3% of the sales price, or you may choose to go it alone without any representation. There won't be any hard feelings. I will wish you well and we will part ways.

The very worst scenario is that you see a for sale by owner home, call them, walk through it, tell them you want to make an offer and then tell them you want to call your real estate agent. I guarantee the seller will be mad. If I try to step in at that point, I will almost always prove to be a hindrance to the negotiations, rather than an asset, because the seller resents my presence.

Some buyers actually believe that they can save money by not using their own agent. They think if there is only one agent, then the seller will have to pay less and be more willing to negotiate on price. I have heard buyers say "by not having an agent, we are saving the seller's 3% and we can get that off the sales price". This attitude shows a basic lack of knowledge of the process.

First, if the sellers are hoping to save the commission on a for sale by owner home, you can't also save that money. There is only one pot of money. At best you could split the difference. But if they already have the home listed with an agent, they are counting on paying that fee. In fact, they are under contract to do so.

Almost all contracts guarantee Broker X a certain commission. That doesn't change if there is no buyer's agent. Broker X just gets twice as much money for themselves. If you ever feel like an agent is trying to pressure you into writing an offer without an agent, now you understand why. The gold mine of real estate is in double ending the deal. It is an ethical tightrope I personally choose not to walk. Sadly, the real losers in this process are typically the undereducated buyer who may end up paying more for the home and do not have an advocate in the inspection process. Not only is a buyer's agent free, but going it alone is just too expensive. A buyer's agent is the best thing you can do to help you in the home buying process.

I wish I could say that all real estate professions have been created equal. Some states still have separate licenses for brokers and agents. If they do, a broker has a great deal more education than an agent which takes very little training to be licensed with that designation. But many states have done away with an agent designation all together. The term 'agent' however, has remained and the two terms, broker and agent, are used almost interchangeably.

Whatever their designation, it is important to find an expert in your area that fits your needs. That may be very different from one person to the next. It is important that you feel comfortable with the person you choose to work with. It doesn't have to be an overly complicated process. You may talk to them by phone, or even email. You may want to meet at their office, or even at a local coffee shop. The most important aspect is that they are able to easily answer your questions, that they know the market and you are comfortable with their level of expertise to guide you through the transaction.

A good buyer's agent should be a source of knowledge and information. They should be striving to educate, to make informed buyers. Be wary of an agent who insists you sign any agreement or contracts to use their services before they have properly acclimated you to the current market conditions. Agents value loyalty and sometimes buyer agreements, something that says if you buy a home it will be done through them, may be necessary to protect an agent from wasted time and resources. But good agents retain clients not because they have locked them into a contract, but because they are a wealth of knowledge that the buyer does not want to be without. A good agent will be a source of referrals for other needed services as well; from home inspectors to electricians to insurance brokers to lenders. Buying a home requires a team and every team needs a good captain.

At this initial meeting, you should get a basic feel for what is available in your prospective price range as well as current market conditions. In a buyers' market, you will have to time look around and take your time. In a sellers' market, you will need to be prepared to act fast when the conditions are right. You should have an idea of some different neighborhoods where homes in your price range can be found, and the age of home you are likely to find.

Learning Your Market

But what if you are not comfortable with the choices you are being shown? Is it time to give up? Absolutely not, but it may be time to adjust your thinking. You may find that you are able to afford more by venturing a little farther out from your target area. You may want to change your search criteria to include different types of homes, like a condo or townhouse instead of a single family home. You may even consider looking at something like a duplex, something with two living units that has the possibility of renting out one unit while living in the other, thus bringing in potential income. Have your searches included financially distressed properties such as foreclosures, or REO (bank owned) properties or short sales? These type of properties will not be a good fit for all buyers, but if you are aware of the potential drawbacks, they could be a great opportunity to get more home for less money.

It is important to know if home values in your area are increasing, decreasing or remaining stagnant. Even more importantly, it is important to know if interest rates are expected to take a drastic drop or sharply increase as this will have a great effect on your purchasing power and may be a factor in the amount of time you want to spend browsing before jumping in and making a real commitment.

If you are not loving the options available to you, consider saving up a larger down payment before buying.

That money down could move you into a price point of home you are more comfortable with.

It may be just as important to take a step back and consider your goals for your first home. Studies in the 2000's showed that first time buyers remained in their home for an average of 5-7 years. During the housing crisis, many buyers lost value and have lacked equity to move on to their next larger purchase, so that number has now expanded to 11-13 years on average. (US Census Bureau, 2010) But with equity on the rise, I would expect to see the number begin to decline again in the near future. It is important to remember this when setting expectations for a home. Too many first time buyers are caught in a trap of expecting to be able to buy what their parents have, right now, right out of the gate. Or they expect to find a home they want to live in for the rest of their lives and raise their family in. It is important to set realistic expectations to make the market work for you. Does the home fit your needs now and for the life you see for yourself in the next decade? Will it appreciate well and help you gain the equity that will be needed to move on to the home of your dreams?

Lending

If after getting an overview of the market you are ready to get serious, it's time to talk lending. You should talk to at least two; one mortgage broker and one lender. A lender is going to work for a bank or credit union, directly. The benefit is that the closing costs are usually lower, but the products offered will be limited to what that bank offers. A mortgage broker works with many different banks and will have a larger variety of loan products to offer, but will have a higher closing cost because there will be a fee for their services.

Online lenders can be a great option for people, but sometimes their distance and lack of knowledge of your specific area can be a problem. Also communication with the team is vital. Online lenders who lack communication skills can slow the process down.

It is important when talking with lenders to understand some basic words, and to make sure you are comparing apples to apples. There will be an interest rate as well as an APR. The APR, or annual percentage rate is a broader measure of the cost of borrowing money. The APR reflects the total cost, such as the interest rate, any discount points, broker fees, and other charges associated in obtaining the loan. When comparing loans, it is important to compare the whole cost of the loan, so comparing APR's rather than interest rates is vital.

Other terms you may hear associated with home loans

Some mortgages may offer **discount points**. This will lower your interest rate, in exchange it will cost you 1% of your loan be paid up front for each point paid down in interest.

Closing costs are often a broad term used for all the costs paid at the closing of the property. These break down into smaller categories. True closing costs are moneys paid in association with the loan like brokerage fees.

Some costs are called **pre-paid costs**. These would include things like discount points, upfront costs for mortgage insurance or a whole year's homeowners insurance premium typically collected at closing.

Pro-rates or pro-rated expenses are costs that are paid for things that are not yet owed, or that are divided between the buyer and seller. Taxes are an easy example of pro-rated expenses. The buyer is only responsible for the property taxes from the day they own the house forward, but a years' worth of taxes will be collected. This cost is pro-rated so the buyer is only paying for their time of ownership.

These items together are commonly referred to as "closing costs".

PMI or Private Mortgage Insurance is required for any private loan with less than a 20% down payment. In general a low down payment puts you in a category of higher risk borrower, and the bank insures your mortgage. Whether is it PMI or MI (government backed mortgage insurance) or an upfront MI premium, if you have a lower than 20% down payment, there will be mortgage insurance on your loan. This will usually be charged monthly in addition to your principle payment and interest.

When analyzing your comfort with your monthly payment it is important to look at the whole payment.

This will include the **Principle**, or the amount owed on the loan, **Interest**, paid on the money borrowed, **Mortgage Insurance**, if you have less than 20% down payment, and money paid into an **impound or escrow account**, or basically a savings account in conjunction with your mortgage that pays your Property Taxes and Homeowners Insurance premiums. If you have a large enough down payment, some banks will not require this type of account, but most will. Banks do this to protect themselves. It insures that your property taxes are paid on time and in full each year to avoid any risk of government foreclosure of the home where the bank may lose money. It also makes sure proper homeowners insurance is provided for the home so, in case of a catastrophic event like a fire where the home is lost, the bank would make sure their investment is safe and a house will be rebuilt. This total monthly payment is often called a PITI Payment, or a PITI +MI, or principle, interest, taxes, insurance plus mortgage insurance. It is the total amount that will be owed each month for your loan payment.

As with real estate brokers, not all lenders are created equal. Talk to friends and family. Listen to the recommendations of your real estate broker. They will know who can get the job done and get the loan done and on time. Most importantly, make sure your lender is an expert in the type of loan you want and that you can communicate well with them.

There are many different kinds of loans and mortgage products. I will highlight some that are frequently used. The most common types of loans are a 30 year fixed loan or a 15 year fixed loan. These are solid loans with very little risk. As a first time buyer, be wary of variable interest rate loans, or adjustable rate mortgages sometimes called ARM loans. You will want to avoid balloon payments, or interest only loans, or loans with a pre-payment penalty, a financial penalty for paying the loan off early if you were to sell the home or refinance. Each of these products serves a purpose, but are usually unsuitable for a first time home buyer.

There are five basic loan options available, with many variations within each product, but I will give a basic overview of each:

VA Loan- this is a product guaranteed by the US Department of Veterans Affairs. Only qualified lenders can underwrite a VA loan. This is for Veterans and their surviving spouses, who have not remarried. A VA loan can be obtained with as little as 0% down, and does not require mortgage insurance. If you are eligible for a VA loan, I would highly recommend you look into that option.

USDA Loan- This loan is designed for rural property owners, but you may be surprised to see what qualifies as rural. This designation is based on local population figures. For some areas, it is not far from a metropolitan center at all. These loans are offered through the US Department of Agriculture and can be as little as 0% down with an upfront mortgage payment premium. There are income caps and home price caps that will apply.

FHA Loan- This is a mortgage insured by the Federal Housing Administration. The loan can have as little as a 3.5% down payment and there is monthly mortgage insurance, until you have paid off 20% of your home, or show that your equity has appreciated to above the 20% mark. FHA has some limits on the types of homes that will qualify for financing, both in condition and type of housing.

Insured Conventional Loan- These are private mortgages with low down payment options, usually 5% or 10%, but private mortgage insurance is still required. Private conventional loans, even with PMI, until 20% of the home is paid off or gained in equity, have less government regulations and provide greater lender flexibility.

Uninsured Conventional Loan- This is the "traditional" mortgage. It requires a 20% down payment and will carry the best interest rates and most flexibility.

Talk with your lender about what type of loan would be best for you. Once you have compared a few loans, you should be issued a pre-approval letter. You cannot actually be approved until you have selected an actual home, but you shouldn't be shopping for what you can't afford. So, a pre-approval is a way of saying that you would qualify once you find the right home.

Stable Pre-Approval

Once you have made the loan application, it is important that your credit remain steady. Do not acquire any new debt. Do not apply for new credit. If there is a change in your income, or hours at work, contact your lender immediately and see if it will affect your ability to make the purchase. Make all your debt payments on time. At this point, something as simple as a late credit card payment could jeopardize the process. It is important to not get so excited about shopping for a home that you forget what you need to do to actually make the purchase.

As you think about the possibility of buying a home, it is important to track your spending carefully over several months. Make sure you know where your money is going each month. This will help you get a handle on how much money you can comfortably allocate to housing expenses. The old adage is that housing should not be more than 28% of your gross (before taxes) monthly income. There is no set federal standard, but that is a good baseline to keep in mind. This ratio of income to monthly payment is often referred to as a front end ratio.

There is another aspect that shows an even more accurate depiction of what you can afford in housing expenses. The back end ratio looks at what percentage of your income is required to cover all your monthly debt obligations. This would include car payments, credit cards, student loans, as well as housing expenses. Some lenders will approve a back end ratio as high as 45%, but ideally 36% or less is a comfortable place to be for most homeowners. Let's try an example:

Tom recently graduated from college and makes $65,000 a year. He's thinking about buying a home, but isn't ready to talk to a real estate broker or lender yet,

Chapter 2
Finding the Right Home

With your market knowledge and pre-approval letter in hand, you are now ready for the fun part. It won't be stress free, but most people enjoy it. There is a reason we hold open houses. It's something in our human nature to be curious about how and where others live. Maybe it lets us fantasize for a little while about what our lives would be like if we lived in each of those places. Maybe we just love shopping. It is the reason I have people tell me, "I'd love to be a real estate broker, to just look at houses all day." In truth, that is maybe 10% of what I do as a real estate broker, but I understand the misconception. As a buyer, it is a huge part of the process. This is your time to shine. You get to pick a home!

Everyone starts out pretty elated, but the actual process of looking for homes can get overwhelming fast. Your real estate broker should be sending you homes that meet your criteria as soon as they hit the market, but there are lots of ways to search for homes. Even when I send every home I can find, it doesn't stop my buyers from browsing the internet on their own. There is so much information at your fingertips. You can search any of the websites and find many of the same properties. Your broker may have their own .search site for you to use. Whatever you choose, use one that is user friendly for you, but be aware that not all of these sites are updated in real time. That means some homes may show up online even after they are sold or under contract. If you are seeing homes that your broker hasn't sent you, you should ask her about them, not just assume that she didn't know they were there. It is possible that she has information that you do not; like perhaps the home will not qualify for the type of lending you are using, or the home may have an accepted contingent offer.

If you see a home that interests you, whether online or driving down the street, call your broker, text him, send him a smoke signal. However you need to communicate with them, do it. But please, make sure you give them an address, or at least a street name. Recently .I received a text from a buyer with a picture of a blue house and the text read "What about this one?" I would like to say that I know every house on the market on sight, but that's just not realistic. And since I am neither clairvoyant nor omnipotent, I had to text back and ask what street she was on. Some hints help us find all the information you need.

Some buyers will browse homes for weeks, even months. Others will take a day. It depends a lot on your temperament and the market conditions at the time. The housing market is cyclical. In the winter there are typically fewer homes listed. The inventory increases in spring and peaks in early summer, then tapers off over fall. When inventory is low, it might take longer to find the right home.

While the home itself is important, there are some other factors to a home that add or detract from its value, both for you and for buyers when you go to sell.

Are there parks in the area? Is there adequate parking? Is the surrounding neighborhood clean and have a low crime rate? Is the neighborhood improving or declining? Think about resale value. This is more than a home. It is an investment in your future and the home's resale value plays a huge roll in that.

There are websites that can give you everything from a list of registered sex offenders in the area to known meth houses, to school test scores, to ethnic breakdowns of the neighborhood. No real estate broker can do all of that research for you. In certain cases it would even be unethical. It is your responsibility to be an educated homebuyer. The information is there for you to find. When you find a home online that peaks your interest, it is time to start looking at the surrounding area and determine what information is important to you. Do not develop tunnel vision because the home itself is attractive to you if everything around it is falling apart.

How many houses should you look at? It depends. I would say at least three. Even the people on reality TV get three to choose from. Most people see between 5-10 homes, but just remember this: more is not always better. Sometimes it just makes it harder to decide what it is you want. And in the process of continued looking, the home you saw eight homes ago, the one you've finally decided was the right one for you, well, someone may have already bought it. If you've looked at 20 or more homes, it's time to re-assess. If you're not finding anything you like, is it because you and your real estate agent aren't communicating well about what you are really looking for? Or is what you're looking for unrealistic in your price or area? Or are you waiting around for the perfect home, when perfect rarely exists?

Here are some tips that might help you know when it is time to write an offer. Before I set out with homebuyers, I ask them to write down the top 10 things they are looking for in a home. Whether that is bedrooms and bathrooms or garage space or a jetted tub, narrow it down to 10. When you walk through a home that meets 7 out of the 10, it is time to start seriously talking about an offer. No home is perfect and short of custom building your dream home, you are not likely to find one with everything you want. The question is; does it have enough of what you want for you to be happy?

Another way to test this is to rate the homes you walk through on a 1-10 scale, 10 being the home of your dreams. Again, when you reach the 7 or so mark, you should think about buying that home.

Some people need to think about it in reverse. For some buyers who may be on the fence I have to ask them this, "If you call me tomorrow and want to write an offer, and I were to tell you that they already accepted another offer, how are you going to feel?" If you would be saddened by missing out on the opportunity, this is a sign that it's time to make an offer.

Writing an Offer

Writing an offer can be intimidating. It is a huge commitment. It may sort of feel like asking a girl to marry you on the first date. You haven't even had time to really get to know her. Unfortunately long term courtship in the real estate world is largely impractical. The good news is that we do believe in long engagements. By the time you have a home inspection and an appraisal over the next few weeks, you're going to have a good feel for all her quirks and hopefully want to marry her still. So don't be afraid. Pull out the ring and get down on one knee, or in this case sit down with a pen and paper, or more likely now with a smart phone or tablet, and take the plunge.

Real estate contracts will vary from state to state, but there are some clauses that are fairly standard, and the process will be similar from market to market. The first thing you must consider is the purchase price. Market conditions in your area will determine how to go about negotiating for a property, but there is one mistake I see first time buyers making all too often.

Somewhere along the line, our culture decided that the price of the home is something to be haggled over, as if going back and forth with offers and counter offers is some sort of rite of passage. Yes, you want to best price for your home, but sometimes nickel and diming over a small amount of money can create animosity that isn't necessary, and that $1000 or $2000 in your mortgage is going to make such a small amount of difference to your monthly payment that it won't even be noticeable. So what are we really haggling over? Remember this; price is not the only item to be negotiated. Don't use all your bargaining power on this one issue. You may need to save some for later.

The next decision is earnest money. At the time that an offer is agreed upon, you will need to give the sellers some money to show good faith. The amount of this deposit will depend on your location and price of the home. A personal check is usually an acceptable form of payment for this. It will be made out to your real estate agent's firm or perhaps the listing agent's firm or the title office, and deposited into a neutral account to be held until the sale closes. At the end of the transaction, this money will be credited towards your down payment or closing costs. When deciding on an amount, you want to make sure it is enough money to be taken seriously, but beware. This is also the amount of money you are willing to lose if the transaction falls apart or you simply change your mind without cause. There are several clauses that will give you a way out of the sale and ensure that you get your earnest money back, but outside of those reasons, if the sale fails, that money goes to the seller.

The most common time for buyer's to change their mind is during the home inspection contingency. This is typically the first 10-15 days of the contract. It is a time for you to hire a home inspector to come in and look at the home in painstaking detail. You are not required to get a whole home inspection, but it will be a few hundred dollars well spent. During this time window, if you find something in the home that you didn't expect, can't feasibly repair or replace or changes the way you think of the house, you may withdraw from the sale and get a refund of your earnest money. You will, however, need to pay for the home inspection. And in some areas you must give the seller to chance to rectify the problem.

Home inspections look at all aspects of the home from the roof and insulation to windows and wiring, but there are some areas that require a special inspection. If the home has a well or a septic system, those inspections will be separate and are vitally important. There is no end to what to test for, but some of the most common are meth testing, lead based paint, asbestos, sewer scopes and radon gas. What additional tests are appropriate for each home will vary. Sometime after a whole home inspection, more specific inspections are needed by a general contractor, electrician or HVAC specialist. Some homes will need repairs. The question is what to ask the sellers to repair before closing, or whether it would be more appropriate to reduce the sales price and have you make the repairs after closing. You will not likely get a perfect home, but this is why using all your negotiating power over price can prove to be foolhardy. This is the second of three opportunities to negotiate with the sellers. Use each wisely. If you have asked for repairs, it is wise to re-inspect those items after the repairs are complete, prior to close and extending any contingency deadlines until you can complete those inspections.

Another contingency in the contract will be an appraisal. If you are getting a loan, the bank will need to verify that the home is worth what you are paying for it. They do this by looking at the sales prices of nearby similar properties. If the appraisal were to come in under your agreed upon price, you have the right to withdraw from the sale and get your earnest money back, but you will likely owe for both a home inspection and an appraisal. This is the third possible negotiating period. It is not always the end of the transaction if the home comes in under value. It can be an excellent way to end up paying less for the house. But the sellers can't be forced to sell their house for a lower price. If you have used up all your negotiating power, you may find yourself in a bad position.

There are many other issues dealt with in the contract. Is the home in a flood plain and will it require flood insurance? There will be so many days for you to obtain a commitment for homeowners insurance. You may want to obtain a survey to determine the exact land boundaries. All of these issues will be dealt with within the contract.

When it is signed, your agent will present your offer. And then… you wait. It is the hardest thing to do. If you are lucky, the sellers will sign it and you will be under contract, but usually there are counter offers, small adjustments here or there to get to a place of agreement.

Chapter 3

The Escrow Process

Once we have an accepted offer you are officially in escrow. I hear people use the term, but few people understand what it means. I personally hate the term, because it is used to mean different things in different situations. The basic concept of Escrow is to place something in the custody of another, or something is to be kept in the custody of another until specific conditions are met. Being "In Escrow" can be the process of closing on a home. It could also be used to mean the actual office that researches title claims and processes the closing papers or it could even mean the account attached to your mortgage that collects property tax and insurance payments. Instead, I would rather not use the word at all, calling it the closing process, a title office, and an impound account.

There are many things that go on in the closing process that remain a mystery for most. There is a lot of paperwork that gets shuffled from place to place that doesn't require too much of the buyer's attention. Most buyers at this point are caught up with the idea of their new home. They are either over the moon about their purchase, spending their time laying out their furniture placement and picking out paint colors, or they may be having a small nervous breakdown. Buying a home is a large financial commitment, the biggest that most will make at one time. It's perfectly acceptable to have some phobia of that kind of commitment. Cold feet happen more often than not. It's okay. Expect it, brace for it. What's important to remember are all the reasons you made an offer on the home in the first place. Talk it through with a trusted advisor. The feeling will usually fade with time. Sometimes the best way to deal with a little case of the jitters is to plunge in to the process and learn more about your home.

There will be a lot of things for you to do in the next month. Let's break the process down, week by week.

Week One

Once an offer is accepted, you need to deliver on the earnest money you offered. How that check is delivered and who it is made out to will vary. Your real estate broker will let you know what to do. Make sure to always note in the memo line what the money is for. For example: Earnest money for 123 Cherry Tree Lane.

In the first few days, sometimes even before you make an offer, you will receive the seller's disclosures, a form with information about the home to the best of the seller's knowledge. Read through them carefully. They are an excellent source of information, from the fuel used for the water heater to any known issues with building permits to boundary issues. Remember that this information is not hard fact, but should be to the best of the seller's knowledge. They are legally culpable if the sellers knowingly leave out vital information on the seller's disclosures.

Work with your real estate broker to set up a whole home inspection and what other inspections you would like to order to take place as soon as possible.

The first week will be focused mostly on providing your lender with all the information needed to begin processing your loan. You will need:

- W-2 or 1099 for the past 2 years along with your federal tax returns
- 3 months of bank statements, all pages
- 2 most recent pay stubs
- Proof of any other income (Tips, Social Security, and Investment income)

There will be other documents as needed for your specific loan and type of employment. It will help the process along if you start collecting these documents early.

Get your lender what they have asked for promptly. Any delays could delay the closing of your home. And remember this. Do not buy anything on credit. Do not take out any new credit. Make all your payments on time. Do nothing that could negatively impact your credit score in any way. It will jeopardize your home purchase. Don't do anything unusual. Don't sell things or buy things. Just pay your bills on time and lay low.

But, moving is expensive, client's tell me. They need to use credit. Never fear! There is a bonus when it comes to your moving budget that most people aren't aware of. In this process, you will likely get what will feel like a month free of rent or mortgage payments. If you were to buy a home on May12th, you would not actually owe anything on your mortgage until July 1. Unlike rent which is paid in advance of each month where a payment made on May 1 pays for May 1-31, mortgages are paid in arrears. With mortgages, a payment made May 1 is actually paying for the previous month, April 1-30. So if you buy a home on May 12, there will be 17 days of prepaid mortgage as part of your closing costs, but you will owe nothing more for May, and make no payment in June as well. It usually is a great help when it comes to planning for those move-in costs and expenses.

In the first week or two, you should be receiving a commitment of Title Insurance on the property. Read over this with your broker and make sure you understand it. This will insure you against any faults in the title, like a long lost brother claiming ownership of the home. Title insurance ensures you have free and clear title to the property, and if there is a claim, you will be refunded up to your purchase price. While title insurance is rarely used, it is important to have. Also, mortgage companies will insist on you providing them with a lenders title policy, to insure their investment.

Week 2

This is likely the time you will complete all your inspections and receive those reports back. Your real estate broker will help you sort through the issues and negotiate needed repairs.

An appraiser will visit the property. They will check to see if the home meets all financing requirements and will assess a value to the home. There may be items the appraiser insists are repaired prior to financing. Hopefully the appraised value of the property you are buying is higher than your purchase price, or at purchase price. If the appraised value is below the agreed purchase price, you and your real estate broker will have to negotiate new terms.

You need to be calling to receive quotes and commitments for homeowners insurance. I recommend starting with your car insurance company as there is typically a discount for bundling policies, but look around at different quotes. Coverage can vary widely, so make sure you are comparing similar policies.

Week 3

This will be a slow week for you in the process while your real estate broker and lender work hard to secure all the needed approvals and documents for the sale. This is the perfect time to pack up and make moving arrangements. It is also the time to file change of addresses with the companies you do business with and with the post office. Contact utility companies and establish service for things like, water, sewer, garbage, gas and electric and call around to select an internet and TV provider.

Week 4

Take the time to pack up your belongings. Make sure, as you pack, that you keep track and separate any financial documents your lender may need at the last minute. Make sure you know where your driver's license or some form of current ID is. You'll need those for when you sign documents.

Closing

This is an exciting, but often stressful time. When the loan documents are returned from the underwriting process you will have approval to close. Those documents then go to the title office and closing statements are prepared. At this point, you will be told the exact amount of money you will need to bring to the signing, and if this can be in a personal check, a wire transfer or cashier's check.

The closing process varies slightly in different areas of the country. In some areas you will come in to sign a couple of days prior to the loan funding and the deed to the property being recorded with the county. You will receive keys to the property when the deed is recorded. In other areas, the signing, funding and recording are done at the same time and you will walk away from the signing table with a hand cramp from repeatedly signing your name on a stack full of documents, as well as keys to your new home.

Whichever way you do it, be prepared to spend an hour in the title office signing paperwork, some of which ranges from key and important to the absurd disclosure of a disclosure of a disclosure of something you signed a month ago. If we are asking you to do it, it is because we are trying to be compliant to all federal laws. We likely find it ridiculous as well, but there's nothing to be done about it, so sign the paper and move on. Many of these documents will need to be notarized, hence the reason for the need for valid ID. The title officer will serve as the notary.

It is easy to get overwhelmed during this last process. If you didn't experience any cold feet earlier, you may have a bad case of them now. Take a deep breath. It's natural. All the reasons to buy a home a month ago have likely not changed. If writing an offer was proposing, this is the wedding ceremony. You're belongings are packed. The guests are waiting. It's time to sign the papers. When the keys are in your hand and you are opening the front door, it will all be worth it.

Chapter 4

Repeat Buyers

First homes are great for what was going on in your life when you bought them, and if you were lucky, you planned ahead for a few years of happiness there, but rarely are first homes your forever home anymore. We change as we age. Our needs change. Whether we've added family members or we just have more belongings, second homes are usually larger and have more living space and storage. I find that people are a little like goldfish. We tend to grow to fit the size of our bowls, and sometimes a new bowl is needed. The question is, when is the right time to upgrade our bowl?

There is no right or wrong answer to that question. Ideally we are told to buy low, and sell high, but what does that even mean in this situation where you will be both a buyer and a seller? In this situation it is best to follow the advice of The Rolling Stones.

> *You can't always get what you want, but if you try sometimes, you might find, you get what you need.*

We are told that we can't have it all; there are few times this phrase will prove to be as true as during this process.

There are other factors that may matter more in determining if this is the moment than just the ebb and flow of the housing market. Maybe you have been offered a better job in another area of the country, or your family needs another bedroom or a yard for your growing family, regardless of the current market. Whatever the reasons, the good and bad of it is that the housing market is rarely neutral. We tend to swing one way or another. You will likely find yourself in either a buyer's or seller's market, which means you are bound to do one side of the deal well, while you will be on the losing end of the other. "Buy high and sell high; or buy low and sell low."

A buyer's market means there are more homes on the market than there are buyers, controlling price, leveraging seller's concessions and putting the buyer's in the driver's seat through the process. A seller's market is the opposite, where there are more buyers than available homes, creating scarcity, elevating prices and enabling sellers to control the transaction. It is critical to understand your current market as those market conditions should dictate how to best move forward.

Whichever market you find yourself in, there is a risk that the timing will not work out in your favor, leaving you either owning two homes, temporarily requiring you to pay two mortgages, or owning no home for a period of time requiring temporary shelter. The process of how to proceed can be overwhelming, keeping some homeowners stuck in neutral. But if you understand the risks involved, you can better prepare to handle them.

Not altogether different from any other home purchase, before you are out and about browsing through potential dream homes, it is important to secure financing, and it will be a little different than it was the first time around. Will you need to sell your existing home first, as it is the source of your down payment? If you purchase a new home before selling your original home, will you qualify for a second home mortgage while still carrying your first? Do you have a down payment without tapping the equity from your first home? Be aware, that if you do decide to buy before selling, the banks will typically want a reserve of up to six months for each mortgage. That means showing enough money in the bank to make both mortgage payments for six months, in addition to your down payment. That can add up fast. Talking to a lender early can help you understand what your options are before heading into the home buying process. You will want to make sure make sure that your loan is secure. Timing in this transaction will be key and you will not be able to afford a slowdown in the mortgage process.

Market Conditions and Timing

If you choose to sell your existing home and find yourself in a ***buyer's market***, use your leverage as a buyer to help you as a seller. Look for your new home first, and when you find it, make an offer contingent on the sale of your current home. This will give you a specific time frame to sell your existing home before moving forward with the purchase. But beware. When you find the right home, you must be prepared to act quickly to get your existing home on the market.

You should have already interviewed real estate brokers and be working with one closely. You should have already gone through your home and made those minor repairs to get the home in top shape. The operating manuals for the appliances or other paperwork that will be needed, such as HOA documents or utility bills should be set aside, organized and ready to go. If it is practical, pictures should be taken for your listing and all listing paperwork filled out and agreed upon. So, when you find the right new home it is as simple as pulling the trigger and your home is on the market as well. Contingent offers are taken much more seriously when the home you are waiting to sell is already on the market and the sellers of your new home can see that your home is in good shape and you are asking a reasonable price.

You are basically asking them to take their house off the market and wait for you. For them to agree to do that, you will need to show that you are serious. When you decide on your list price for your existing home, remember that time on the market is going to be more important than final sales price. You will not be able to get both. With your real estate broker, look at the target price range and choose a price on the lower end of the range. If you price it right, even in a buyer's market, you may be able to attract multiple buyers and then you can allow them to raise the price amongst themselves, and you may choose the offer with the best terms for you, which would be a quick close and stable, secure financing.

If your existing home does not sell in time, the sellers of your new home will ask that you remove the contingency, either moving forward with your purchase or withdrawing and allowing them to put their home back on the market. If you are financially able, you may choose to proceed with the purchase, and in the end, you will likely, all be it temporarily, be the owner of two homes. If you are not financially able to proceed with the sale, you will need to withdraw, and you may lose the home you had been dreaming of.

The formula is different if you are in a ***seller's market***. In a seller's market you should consider listing your existing home for sale first. Again, you need to leverage the side of the transaction where you have the power. As the seller, you may have multiple offers and be able to make the purchase contingent on the close of the purchase of your next home. Remember, in a seller's market, there are fewer homes to choose from and you cannot reasonably expect buyers to hang around forever. You will likely only be able to buy yourself a few weeks to select a new home and get it under contract. The risk here is that you will not find what you like in that time frame, in which case you can terminate the sale of your existing home, or proceed with that sale and find temporary housing until the right house comes along.

When listing your home, price will again be key. It will be easier for you to get what you want as far as contingencies if there are multiple offers on the home. You must decide which is most important to you, top dollar or timing. You likely cannot have both.

As you look at potential new homes, remember a few things. You are now the buyer and in the weaker position, so you will need to write a strong offer to be competitive. This likely doesn't mean a full price offer, or that you have to give away the bank, but be realistic for the market. Look at other comparable sales in the area.

The seller's certainly have. If you all know what the reasonable sales price will be, don't start so low that you draw out the negotiation process. Offer, counter offer. Anything more than that is prolonging the inevitable and may cost you the home if another potential buyer arrives on the scene.

Condition

You should also keep an eye out for potential issues or delays. If the home were to need a new roof in order to finance, your closing process is extended for however long a roof takes to put on, impacting the sale of your existing home as well. You are not a home inspector and shouldn't think that you can find every potential problem in a home, but there are warning signs you can look for in any home that may give you a heads up of potential trouble ahead.

- **GRADING**: If the home has dirt or yard sloping down towards it, it has the possibility of serious water intrusion issues. Grading and sloping are easy to see in all seasons. Perhaps the home will be dry when you are looking at it, but may not have been last winter. Look for large cracks in the foundation or areas that show signs of water pooling.

- **MOISTURE**: Look for discoloration and stains around the base of the home's foundation, as well as inside the home and on the walls around the home. Look for stains on the ceiling. Small bulges or stains can be signs of a roof leak or plumbing leak. Especially in basements or corners of rooms with less ventilation look for mold growth. Be aware of bowing or bubbling of the flooring that could be caused by moisture damage as well.

- **APPLIANCES**: A new fridge or stove shouldn't be a deal breaker, but a new furnace or air conditioning unit may be a different story. Take the time to look them over, see if they have been properly maintained, and if they seem to be old or in disrepair.

- **ROOFING**: A roof is crucial to keeping a home safe and dry. If the shingles look warn, if there is marked discoloration in areas or obvious patchwork, be leery. Look at the gutters. Are they in place? Are they clogged and leaking? Clogged gutters can send water back under the roofline causing wood rot under the shingles.

- **GENERAL DEFERRED MAINTENANCE**: Whether it is exposed wood that should have been painted over, a worn roof or clogged gutters, a home that has not been properly maintained will show it, if you look. They call it deferred maintenance for a reason. The problems will not go away; you can only put them off for a while. If you are not prepared to take on those maintenance issues, a poorly maintained home, at any price, will not be a bargain.

Being aware of these issues will not guarantee a clean home inspection, but it may help prevent some wasted time in a process where time will very rarely be your friend. Upgrading homes is like a carefully coordinated dance. Hopefully, if you know the choreography, the steps will be easier to follow. But it is important to set reasonable goals and not get distracted from those goals during the negotiation processes, something you will endure on both transactions. I try not to take too many life lessons from classic rock ballads, but this one is a sure bet.

You can't always get what you want.
But if you try sometimes, you might find, you get what you need.

Quick Buyer Review

As humans, when we only do something every 5-10 years or more, it is almost impossible for us to remember all the steps to perform the task. It is no different in real estate. That is one of the many reasons it is important to have an expert by your side, someone who does it every day. And because you do not, it is perfectly acceptable to need a bit of a refresher course. I have spent a considerable amount of space talking about the process of buying a home in the previous section of this book, but a brief recap may be useful.

As was discussed in the previous chapter, financing is key. Talk with at least one direct lender and one mortgage broker. Compare different types of loans and the APR for each rather than a flat interest rate which can be deceiving.

Once you have secured financing, you want to determine areas that are reasonable and desirable to you. Work with your real estate broker to explore all the options that fit your needs. Your broker should be sending you listings as soon as they hit the market. Most upgrading buyers have a fairly good idea of what they are looking for and typically look at fewer homes than they did the first time around.

Once an offer is written and accepted, earnest money will be paid. In the coming weeks a home inspection and appraisal will be complete, and when the loan documents are ready, there will be a signing, funding, and recording. More about this process is laid out earlier in this book including a checklist of what to expect and what needs to be accomplished each week of the escrow process.

Quick Seller Review

What it takes to sell your home is covered later, but a quick overview of key factors will help you get on the right track. There are lots of things that need to be done to properly sell your home, getting you the best possible price for your situation and timeline. Using a professional real estate broker will statistically net you a higher sales price and shorten your time on the market.

Hiring a professional to market your home will not relieve you of all responsibilities however. A property must be prepped. Everything your mother ever told you about first impressions is doubly true about a house's debut on the market. Take an extra day and do it right.

The home needs to be clean and odor free. Even a well-kept home will benefit from a deep clean prior to listing. Prior to the house hitting the market, you want to take a moment and touch up the small dings and scrapes that life causes.

Don't give any buyer a reason to worry that the house is poorly maintained. Sometimes we become blind to those sorts of nicks and scuffs that are there every day. It would be beneficial to walk the property with your real estate broker and see what their trained eye is drawn to, for good or bad.

This is also the time to remove the clutter. Take down personal pictures. Put away the kid's artwork on the fridge. Replace dimming light bulbs. Get rid of wiring from electronics that may be dangling about. Empty seasonal items not in use from the closets. The goal is to make the home appear as open and bright as possible. Sometimes this means moving some furniture around, or moving some pieces out of the house all together. If it is practical, and in your price range, your real estate broker may have a home stager come in and optimize the look and feel of the home.

When the house is being shown, it will be important to straighten up and get it in "showing" condition. No dirty dishes in the sink. Take the trash out. Clean up the scattered toys from children. Empty the cat litter, or anything else that might cause an unpleasant odor. But also avoid air fresheners. They can be overwhelming in a home and be a sign of an odor that is being masked. If you want to add a fresh scent, you may consider tucking a fabric softener sheet in a drawer in the bathroom, or a box of baking soda in the fridge. (Yes, they will open your fridge). These absorb odor and have a natural, more neutral scent.

You will also need to secure your personal items. The most common items stolen from homes in open houses or showings are jewelry and prescription drugs.

Either lock them up, tuck them way out of sight, or take them with you.

It is not that other real estate agents or even yours, would knowingly let people steal from you, but you are inviting strangers into your home. You *need* strangers to come into your most intimate spaces. So, protect yourself.

Upgrading your home will not be stress free, but the benefits of a home that better suits your needs will make it worth it. This will more likely be the home you live in for 10-20 years or more. It will likely be the home you raise your family in. This is a real grown up home and it will appreciate like one. Make it a home you are comfortable in, and have room to grow with a lifestyle that will continue to evolve as you and your family grow. Thinking about things like schools and recreation will become critical.

Are You Ready to Be a Real Estate Investor?

If you do have the kind of money on hand to cover a new mortgage as well as your existing home for 6 months, you should probably be considering another option. Rather than selling your existing home, perhaps it would make a good rental property, turning your first home into your first investment property. To determine if this is a good fit for you, you will need to have access to information about your current rental market in addition to your real estate market. Not all real estate brokers have experience with investment properties. Find one who does, who can guide you through the process. If you are in a solid rental market, have a way to oversee the property yourself or have a management service, and can rent it for at least what you owe monthly, it may make sense to jump into investment real estate here, in a comfortable area for you. You may even be able to use some of the equity in that home toward your future purchase or reserve. You can do this by obtaining a HELOC or Home Equity Line of Credit on your existing home, but this must be done while it is still your primary residence. Investment properties are all but impossible to get a second mortgage on. HELOC's can provide financing up to 90% of your home's value in mortgages, allowing you to pull all but 10% of equity from your home to help with a new purchase.

There are other questions to consider, such as; is the size and area of your home located desirable for renters? Do you know or can you brush up on rental laws and regulations in your area and can you reasonably set money aside to cover vacancies, repairs and maintenance to the home? For some, this will prove to be the easiest way to transition from owning a home to true investments in real estate. In this scenario, what may only pay the mortgage now, with rental rates climbing, will eventually serve as monthly income, and the equity will continue to accrue in the property, as well as the tax benefits of ownership, thereby increasing your personal wealth.

If you are financially able to retain your first home as a rental, you have taken the first step into investment real estate and will begin to build your personal wealth in ways that can't be done by simply owning your personal residence.

Investing in Real Estate

Chapter 5

Types of Investments

Successful investments in real estate can be accomplished in many different ways, but they all have one thing in common. It is something done with a strategy. There must be a plan for what you want to accomplish before you ever get started. There are times that people find an interesting property, something that appears to be a good deal and they want to jump on it before the opportunity is snapped up by someone else; however jumping in before you have a plan for that property and can adequately evaluate the strategy for the property is setting yourself up for failure. It is simply putting the proverbial cart before the horse.

Investment is not about whether or not you like a home or whether you could see yourself living in it, or whether it would suit your needs. In that way, it varies greatly from other real estate transactions. It is not an emotional decision, or shouldn't be. When investing in real estate it is best to take a step back from all your emotions and evaluate the numbers. Get the best market estimates and evaluations that you can find and analyze the numbers rationally.

Know your investment strategy. There are long term and short term investment strategies. What is it that you are looking for in a potential investment property? Whether it is income or equity or tax relief, you need a property that can provide it for you. You will need to realistically look at what is reasonable for your situation, your down payment and what you can provide to buy into the investment. Short term real estate investments can, in certain markets, yield high rewards, but carry much greater risk than a long term investment would. Longer investment strategies are safer, less risky, and have the potential for high reward in the long term, but may not show any profit for many years to come.

While most people think of property ownership as residential real estate, there are many other forms that ought to be considered. Which is right for you will vary depending on your situation, your risk tolerance level, and your ultimate goals for your investment. While residential rental property is certainly the oldest and most traditional real estate investment, there are other ways to go about it.

There are real estate investment groups. These groups are managed much like a mutual fund, but rather than owning stocks they own real estate, usually in multiple forms in multiple markets. There is typically a high buy in cost and you will have no control over what it is you are purchasing. It is a hands off investment, so it is very important to research the group and its management before making any decisions on what group may be right for you. The group will only be as successful as the management and the investments they choose with their existing investment strategy.

Similar to investment groups is tenants in common property. This is usually a large office building, or a similar arrangement called a REIT or a real estate investment trust. This allows you to purchase stock in the trust, or in a TIC, a share. The costs of management are divided equally amongst the owners as well as repairs and vacancies and profits are paid according to the companies rules. Unlike an investment group, you will likely have a good idea of what you are buying, but you will not have the control or responsibility for day to day decisions about the property.

Short term investment strategies typically involve flipping in one way or another. Whether it is a financially distressed home that is turned in the same condition, hoping for a profit, or a fixer upper where improvements are made to gain equity and then sold, it is a "flip" home and carries a high risk. The same is true for the less traditional forms such as purchasing land and dividing it to its highest and best use, then selling it to a developer or developing it yourself and selling off the individual pieces, or even buying an existing building and parceling off each part, perhaps a duplex that can be sold as individual townhomes with minor modifications and approval from local governing agencies.

For our purposes, we are going to concentrate on the risks and benefits of more traditional investment rental situations. They are the most common first investment. They allow a low pay in and the ability to leverage, or obtain a mortgage. Within that category of investment, there are even more options. Residential investment is categorized as a private residence between 1-4 units. This could be a single family home that you intend to rent out, or a duplex with two rental units on the same lot of land, a triplex with three rental units on the same lot of land or a 4 plex. This is an excellent place to begin for most first time investors because the costs are low, and the rules governing the rental are familiar as they are similar to those for residential homeowners.

When there are more than five rental units the project is categorized as a commercial residential real estate purchase, changing the types of loans that are available, as well as the government regulations and oversight. In the eyes of the law, this is now a business, and will be treated as one. Financially, and with many regulations, it is the same as a commercial rental, such as an office space or a strip mall, or even a hotel. There will be more regulations about things like garbage and recycling and smoke detectors, even sprinkler systems. With more units comes more value, but the buy in cost is usually higher. While they certainly have advantages, it is not typically the place people start investing in real estate.

With a residential rental property, obtaining a loan will be relatively easy. You will need to qualify for the mortgage and show a reserve which is usually six months' worth of mortgage payments set aside. This can be in a 401k or other type of investment account. It does not have to be cash on hand. It will be a traditional 20% down conventional loan, though the interest rate will likely be higher on a non-owner occupied property. Once you know what you can feasibly buy, the question is what are you looking for?

Cap Rate and Gross Rent Multiplier

There are many strategies used to determine what investment may have the best potential for you. I will define only two that are commonly used by real estate professionals to help analyze potential investments.

Capitalization rates, usually simply referred to as cap rates are best used to analyze what type of investment would be financially advantageous for you. In its most simple term a cap rate is found by dividing the net operating income by the current market value of the property. If you were considering buying an apartment building worth $1,000,000 and the net operating income (all collected rents minus operating expenses) was $72,000, the cap rate would be 7.2%.

Cap rates are a way of showing the rate of return on a real estate investment based on the income the property is expected to generate. Essentially the cap rate gauges profitability of a given investment, but cap rates have their faults. They can be overly simplistic and therefore deceiving. For instance, if your $1,000,000 apartment building was in a rapidly appreciating market, and suddenly increased in value to $1,500,000, but rents lagged behind because rental increases are done but once a year and rents cannot appreciate at the same rate without causing mass vacancies and therefore lost revenue, suddenly your cap rate has dropped to 4.8%, a much less desirable number which would indicate for some investors to sell and put their money in a more lucrative investment. If, however, patience was applied and modest rental increases were made over the next year, the cap rate would rise to 5.8% and continue to rise and rental values increased.

The biggest problem with cap rates is that they are meant to project an estimated return on an investment in an all cash transaction (which most are not), where market values remain constant, (which they rarely do) and where net operating income remains level, (which it is not likely to do in a rental situation). So, what is this mysterious number good for? Cap rates are best used to compare one type of investment to another. Would a single family rental home have a better or worse return over an apartment building? What about residential investment vs. commercial? The higher the cap rate-the better the theoretical investment for you as opposed to lower risk type investments.

I recommend that buyers set a minimum acceptable cap rate, the rate where the additional risk would be worthwhile. For instance: let's say you could buy a US Treasury bond with a 3% return. Most people would consider this a zero risk investment. Short of a government collapse or a national credit melt down, those funds are guaranteed, unlike a rental home where you may encounter vacancies like water heaters dying, roofs needing replacing, or potential damage done by tenants such as a destructive pet or a tenant who cooked methamphetamines. Of course you can try to mitigate those risks by tenant screening and budgeting for foreseeable repairs, but nothing can completely absolve you of risk. And while more units increase income, it also increases risk. In a 4 plex you may have four times the rent, but you have four times the bathrooms and kitchens to develop leaks, four times the water heaters and four times the possibility of vacancies. So the question becomes: "at what point is the increased return worth the risk?" If the zero risk investment yields a 3% cap rate, would a 5% cap rate make the risk worthwhile? Is it 8%? Or 10%? That's a question best answered by each individual investor with their own tolerance level for risk and reward. If that number were to be 6%, then you need to compare different types of investments on the market to see what is available to you in that range or better and use the cap rate to select the highest and best investment for you in your circumstances.

Once you have decided on a type of investment and you are comparing investments of the same type (duplexes, for example) it is best to move beyond the cap rate to a method that better compares alike investments. It is the Gross Rate Multiplier. It is simply the sales price divided by the annual rents (or potential income). For example, if there is a 4 plex with all four units renting for $800 a month, the gross potential rent for the year would be $38,400. If the building was listed for sale at $300,000, the GRM would be 7.81.

The GRM or gross rent multiplier aids in comparing like investments in the same area. Let's continue the example of the building mentioned above. It has four units renting for $800 a month and is listed for $300,000. If a neighboring building had four units renting for $925 and is listed for $412,000 it may not be readily apparent which the better buy is. Yes, the second building costs more, but it also collects more in rent. Comparing gross rent multipliers consolidates those figures into one easy to understand number. The first building's GRM is 7.81. The second's is 9.28. The lower the gross rent multiplier, the better the buy. In this example, the first building requires less money up front and collects more rent in relation to the purchase price.

Gross rent multipliers also work in reverse. You can take the annual perspective rent and multiply it by the gross rent multiplier you are looking for and come up with a purchase price. To continue our example, if you could purchase building two, with its perspective annual rent of $44,400, for a purchase price of $346,764, then it would be an equal buy with building number one. The GRM is also useful when preparing to sell an investment property to make sure your investment is priced correctly in comparison to other similar properties in regard to the rental income. If the seller of building number two wants to be competitive with their neighbor, assuming the buildings are in similar condition, they will need to significantly reduce their price.

Statistical analyses such as cap rates and gross rent multipliers are tools used to determine the use and value of potential assets, but they cannot replace good logic or account for every factor that can go into determining the best property for you. They cannot assess your level of comfort with risk. They cannot tell you the condition of properties or accurately assess other factors such as tenant stability and turnover costs.

If you have determined that building number one in our example is the better buy, the next question you should be asking yourself, if you were comparing these two properties, is why a neighboring property is able to rent a unit for $125 more a month than building number one. Does building two have extra ammonites offered to the tenants? Does building one have deferred maintenance issues? Will it cost you a significant amount of money to improve the building to a level that will tolerate the higher rental amount? Are there long term tenants in the building that have allowed rents to fall well below market value? It is an all too common situation in buildings on the market. The owner has allowed rents to fall below market value, dropping their cap rate to a point below their benefit vs. risk point, thereby making it no longer a desirable investment for their money.

What does that mean for you as a buyer? If the market rent is really $925, and you were to raise your rents to fair market value, you run the risk of mass vacancies, bringing not only loss of rent, but also costs like carpet replacement, painting and other routine turn over expenses. Tenants do not usually take kindly to rental increases of that size all at once. So you must consider how you would go about raising rents to the desired level. If market rents are really $925 and your perspective units are renting at $800, could you raise them to $850 this year and $900 the next and $950 the year after that, which should bring you fairly in step with rental inflation in the area? Could you do that and keep the existing tenants in place saving you the turn over expenses? Do you in fact *want* to keep the existing tenants at all?

Tenant Screening

Tenant screening is a huge issue in order to mitigate risk. When you are buying a building with renters in leases, those leases carry over to your ownership. If the lease is vague in scope and wording, you inherit the problems left behind by less involved owners. If tenant screening was done poorly, or not at all, you inherit the last owner's problems. You will want to ask for documentation of rental payments made over the last year and any written warnings, complaints or notices issues in the tenant's rental history. You should tour each unit. This is typically done after an offer is accepted but before a professional inspection of the property or appraisal. Tenants are typically given at least 24 hours' notice of the visit and will have cleaned up their unit. Consider this condition to be the tenants at their best. If the way they live at their best is alarming to you, understand that it is likely to only get worse after you become the owner and you will incur the costs of turning over the unit with any damage the tenants have done. Sometimes a building with vacancies can be more attractive than below par tenants in a lease that you cannot terminate.

As part of the closing process, make sure you have an accurate accounting of all deposits that would be refundable to tenants in the future, that it matches the written leases, as these funds will be transferred to you at closing. If it is not accounted for properly in the closing process, the tenant still has a right to the return of that money from you after they vacate. You do not want to have to pay out money that you did not collect.

Once your inspection is complete, the purchase process is not altogether different from buying a home. There should be a professional inspection and an appraisal done. Loan docs will be drawn up and moneys will be exchanged at closing. You will need to set up default accounts for the utilities of vacant units, as you would set up utilities for your own home and you will need to notify the tenants as to how and where they are to pay their rent after closing. Keys to the units should be up to date and exchanged at closing along with any other items that may have been included in the contract. Copies of rental agreements should have been delivered in the first few days of the contract period, but if they have not, they should be provided now.

For more commercial applications, the process will vary slightly, but it is still true to look over leases and revenue history. You will have to consider additional issues like trade fixtures and uses. But the tests of cap rate and gross rent multipliers are still an effective quick tool to amylase and compare investments. And other items hold true across investment formats.

One of my most crucial truths is this: low rents benefit no one. They effectively lower your property value, as your cap rate falls and gross rent multiplier rises. Lower rents cause a negative cash flow from the building, leading to deferred maintenance which is bad for the building's value and decreases rentability. The best thing you can do as an owner for your building's long term stability is to keep your rents near market value, compensating for location and available amenities. In a competitive market you may want to be 5% under market value. In our example of a unit renting for $925, that would mean a rental rate of $880 a month. Lower than that has negative implications for the building, the tenant's quality of life and your financial stability. Consistent, small rental increases should be used to keep up with healthy inflation, and always consider turn over expenses when considering a larger to moderate rental increase.

When looking at buildings it is important to consider the benefits and drawbacks of amenities offered. In unit laundry hook ups a nice, but would you provide the washer and dryer, adding appliances that could break and need replaced? An onsite laundry facility has the potential of generating income but also comes with the expense of machine upkeep and security issues. Pools and playgrounds will allow you to charge higher rents because tenants find these amenities desirable, but the upkeep costs can be high, as well as insurance costs for liability issues.

Whatever type of investment property you decide on, make sure you diversify your investing. Just as no one would recommend you putting your entire 401K into a single company's stock, diversifying real estate portfolios brings greater financial stability. Diversifying can be across markets and across areas of real estate, but you are more likely to find success if you stick within your comfort zone. If your comfort zone is residential real estate, look at single family homes, as well as duplexes and multi-plexes. If you only want single family homes, consider buying in your current area and look at investments in different real estate markets in the country. You will find very different markets in San Francisco vs. Omaha, Portland vs. Bloomington. If something were to happen to affect the Portland housing market, it will not necessarily affect appreciation or depreciation of Bloomington, Indiana. If the rental market of Omaha is devastated by the loss of several large businesses, it is likely that your investments in San Francisco are still stable. This diversification allows for long term stability, built over time as your financial wealth builds.

Chapter 6
Managing Rental Properties

The single best way to mitigate your risk as a property owner is to be, or to employ, active managers. Tasks for managers include making a long and short term maintenance plan for the building, keeping an eye on tenant behavior issues, collecting rents and managing accounts, advertising units for rent and screening prospective tenants.

Professional management is not free and good professional management won't be cheap. Expect to pay 10%- 15% of the collected monthly rents to a professional management firm in addition to repair or maintenance expenses usually charged above the rental percentage. This will provide you all- inclusive management, including access to handyman services and vendors like carpet cleaners and painters. Professional managers should be able to assess the building and provide you with a long term budget for future repairs and alterations. You will want and need the tax write offs of capital expenditures, but you may not want them all done in the same year, costing you money out of pocket. It is important to predict things like roof replacements, and budget for possible needed improvements like new windows or air conditioning. There should also be a projected budget for the unforeseen expenses such as appliances breaking and a plan for what updates will be done to each unit as they are turned over. They will likely have their own document package with a strong lease agreement and thorough applicant screening process. In this, as in many other areas, you may get what you pay for. An unreputable management company may be worse than no manager at all. Professional management will reduce more of the owner's daily responsibility and allow you to manage your investment from a more financial perspective rather than the day to day issues of owning a building. For many owners, professional management is worth the cost. It will also give you the value of expertise and experience.

For larger complexes, an on-site manager may be a more practical option. Usually for discounted rent, they will show vacancies and handle tenant issues. However it is imperative to find the right person or family to represent you and set clear expectations. Typically on site managers do not have professional training or experience, so their scope will be limited to basic services.

Self-management is also an option for an owner who wants a more hands on experience in their investment. If you choose this route, you will want to maintain a certain amount of anonymity for your own protection. Do not have tenants mail checks to your personal address, or meet you at your home. When relationships go bad with tenants, they tend to go very bad. Keeping your distance will bring a certain level of peace of mind when tenants become problems. You should not attempt to go at it alone without a vast amount of experience or the assistance of experts. A good lawyer familiar with rental law and evictions is a must. They can help you set up a basic package of notices, such as pay or quit or perform or quit, applications and rental agreements that follow all local and state laws while protecting your interests as an owner. A strong lease will go a long way in protecting your long term best interests. Make sure it addresses items such as sub-leasing and roommates. A solid practice would be to require anyone over the age of 18 to be on the lease and subject to tenant screening. With other people living in the property, you lose control over enforcing rules and regulations; in addition to control over what type of people inhabit your property. The lease should also address issues like animals and smoking. It must be compliant with all regulations of the American with Disabilities Act and other local rules. Also carefully review your insurance rider for information regarding disabled smoke detectors. In many cases damages caused by a fire may not be covered if there is evidence that a tenant tampered with or removed smoke detectors. This is something that should be addressed in the lease. There must also be a discussion of late fees, fees and deposits. Deposits are by definition refundable when certain conditions are met, which must be clearly stated in the contract. Fees are nonrefundable.

When you are ready with a strong document package, it is time to put policies in place. Self-management means being actively involved in listing properties for rent in your market, screening tenants, signing leases and collecting funds. If that is not something you can commit to, do not do yourself the financial disservice of trying to manage your own building just to save some money. It will end up costing you in the long run. If you are ready for the challenge, consider the following issues:

There are four items that should always be checked when screening new applicants. They are a criminal background check, a credit check, and employment verification and rental references. There are many agencies that can run a credit and criminal search online for a fee. The application fee should at least cover those costs. Employment verification can be done by contacting their employer to verify income. A prospective tenant should make at least three times the rent in income monthly to lower your risk of default. In a credit check, you may run into issues of young or underused credit. That does not mean that would be a bad tenant. Even a recent bankruptcy should not necessarily preclude a tenant. What you are looking for is a pattern of financial instability. Do they have multiple accounts in collections in different areas? Is it medical bills and utilities and credit cards? Have they had cars repossessed? This shows a pattern of them not paying bills and should reasonably be avoided. The preferred rental reference is not from the current landlord who may not want to lose a tenant or may want to desperately be rid of them, but rather from a previous landlord who has no stake in the outcome and can give you an honest overview and history including how the tenant left the property. It is important to ask questions they can answer. Professional managers are bound by professional ethics. Make your questions objective and fact based. Being professional in what you ask will usually get you a professional response.

Having a good working relationship with tenants is vital for effective management. It is important that they know that your answers are consistent and policies will be enforced. Penalties need to be clearly stated and stuck to. Those may include parking issues or late fees. There is a way to be strict without being unreasonable, enabling a good working relationship to continue even in times of trouble. But there may be times where reason is no longer a feasible option. Some tenants will push and push past the point of all reason or even sanity. When put in that situation, remember that it is better to be sane than right. Sometimes getting the situation over with is worth the loss of rental revenue, and can be less costly than an expensive eviction. When in a difficult situation with a tenant where you may want them off the property, before you contact your attorney to evict the tenant, try to negotiate a mutual release from the contract. They move, you do not seek future rents owed in the terms of the lease. Move on. Make it easy for everyone to move on. Sanity has more value than any monetary prospects, because regardless of the best screening practices, eventually, you will get that one tenant, the one you tell stories about for years to come. The good news is, usually they are good for a laugh with friends, once the people are off your property.

Chapter 7

Financially Distressed Properties

Whether it's people looking for their own home or investors looking for a deal, I often am asked about distressed properties, both in condition or financially. But while the term foreclosure is familiar to most people, there seems to be some confusion about the process and how people can go about purchasing a foreclosed home. The advent of online sites that include pre-foreclosure homes has only added to the confusion.

You may see a home on a website listed as a pre-foreclosure. This means that the owner is behind in their mortgage payments. It does not in any way indicate that the house is available or on the market or that the owner is the least bit interested in selling their home, though if they are in financial straits, it may be a wise decision for them. It may indicate a value, but that value could be anything from an online estimate, (famed for its inaccuracy) to the former purchase price or original mortgage amount, or even an estimate of what the owner now owes. So take the information with a grain of salt. If you are truly interested in the property, there is nothing wrong with you or your agent reaching out to the owner and asking if they are interested in selling, but do not be overly optimistic about the response you might receive. Financial loss causes its own grief and some stages of grief are denial and anger. You may find a receptive and reasonable seller, but you are just as likely to be greeted by someone who is angry, embarrassed, and determined that they don't need anyone's help. And even if they did, they are likely being contacted by the bottom feeders of the real estate world giving them conflicting information about how, for a price, they can save their home or restructure their mortgage. They are often confused and do not know who to trust of where to go for accurate information. For those who do choose to sell, they may list their home on the open market where some buyers will not even be aware of their financial distress. Other sellers will be underwater, meaning they owe more on their home than what it is currently worth. In that case, if they cannot maintain the current mortgages payment structure, they have limited options. They can try to work with the bank (if they are willing) to renegotiate or restructure their existing mortgage, they can let the bank foreclose on the home, or they can try to negotiate a short sale.

The term short sale has fostered some rather unfortunate misunderstandings. Several years ago I received a call about one of my short sale listings. It was a potential buyer with a question. It became clear that this home was not what they were looking for and I asked if they would be interested in seeing other homes that might better fit their needs. The buyer then told me, "Okay, but we're only looking at short sales because I'm about to have a baby and we want to be able to move in before the baby comes." Much to her dismay, I had to explain that short does not equate to fast. It means that the sellers are shorting the bank money, not repaying the whole loan amount and we have to negotiate with the bank to have them write off the remaining amount as a loss. Nothing about a short sale is fast. In fact it can take months to years to work with banks to get them to agree on a sales price and how to deal with the remaining debt. The complication of the process only grows when there is more than one bank involved or more than one mortgage. In a down market, short sales become more common and there can be some great deals to be had, but bring a suitcase full of patience and a pocket full of time.

    Some wonder why banks would agree to a short sale at all. It is a simple math problem, really, and it makes more sense when you realize that foreclosing by a bank is not free. In fact it is an incredibly expensive process for a bank to foreclose, list, and sell a home. It can cost a bank between $50,000 and $100,000 for the bank to buy back the home. To illustrate why a short sale may be attractive to a bank, let's take a look at Stan.

    Stan bought his home in 2007 at the height of the market at $300,000 with a mortgage amount of $285,000 and a payment of $1785 a month. From 2007-2010 Stan's home lost value in the national housing crisis, nearly 25% of its value. But in 2016 his home value has increased again and his home is now worth $236,000. But Stan is faced with his work changing. The firm is closing its local office. He will need to transfer out of state or be out of work. As of 2016, his mortgage payoff was $243,000. If Stan were to sell his home at the best possible price of $240,000 with closing fees and other costs, Stan would be short by over $20,000. Stan does not have $20,000 to give to the bank at closing, so he has a choice. He can try to short sale his home, which will hurt, but not destroy his credit rating, or simply move on and let the bank take the house, devastating his credit. Stan opts to try to short sell the home. But why would the bank? The numbers are still accurate. The bank is owed $243,000 and at most can sell the home for $240,000, likely less because it is financially distressed. But if the bank were to foreclose, they would incur legal fees of at least $50,000 and loss of mortgage payments for at least a year. And when it is all over, they would be in debt $300,000 on a home they can still only sell for no more than $240,000. Therefore a foreclosure loss would be $60,000 and a short sale loss would be $20,000. A short sale, in this scenario is exactly $40,000 more attractive to the bank.

If a home does go into foreclosure there are many steps that are taken before the house appears on the MLS with a for sale sign in front. Once the foreclosure judgement is issued, there must be a public auction. These are sometimes held on the courthouse steps, called a courthouse auction, though they may be in any location designated by the court. In this process, the bank usually sets a reserve bid, a high amount they will pay to buy the home. If they are outbid, anyone may purchase a home at a courthouse auction, but it will not be like any other home purchase you will see. First, you had better bring your checkbook, because you will be expected to pay for the house, then and there. You will likely never have set foot in the house, and you will have no inspection period or appraisal period. When the court says sold, that's it, with one exception. In some states the original owner has a right of redemption, a number of days they may remain in the house, or pay off the bank and maintain the rights to their home. It is unusual for a homeowner to use this redemptive period, but it happens, and in the meantime you have a very unhappy tenant in your home. There are lists you can buy of these courthouse auctions, but these auctions are not for the faint of heart or bank account. There is the potential for huge windfalls, but just as likely, huge losses. The home may require a new roof. It may have been stripped of all wiring; it may have a faulty foundation. The unknowns outnumber the knowns. This style of courthouse action is a game for the big kids and no first time investor of any kind belong there. Wet your feet in a more friendly pool. This would be akin to jumping into a shark tank. These are the deals well suited for the investor who will not be negatively affected by losing significant amounts of money on 2-4 bad deals a year. Don't play with what you can't afford to lose. Yes, this is a high reward scenario, but with it comes huge risks. There are no safety nets in this process for the buyer.

Assuming the bank wins the home at the courthouse auction, the home would then enter the bank's asset rolls. While there, it may be purchased in a bulk sale, such as a mutual fund or other investment account. If not, it will eventually be assigned to a real estate broker who works for the bank, called an REO agent. At this point the bank can take one of two routes. One option is that they can list it as a traditional sale. You may tour it, write an offer on the standard paperwork, pay earnest money, get a home inspection and appraisal, and purchase it with whatever home loan might be appropriate. The bank itself may even offer special financing incentives. The main difference between this and a traditional purchase is what you see is likely what you get. The bank will be exempt from any disclosure forms concerning the home's condition, and the bank will usually make no repairs, unless there is something specified by the agreed upon lending, such as a furnace that needs to be replaced in order for you to obtain your loan. Banks know what is needed for lending and typically take care of those issues before listing the home. If you are looking at foreclosures or REO listings as they are sometimes referred to, I urge you to get a thorough home inspection. I have seen angry homeowners do horrible things like pouring kitty litter down drain pipes and pouring chemicals on the lawn to kill the grass. They are angry and want to stick it to the banks on their way out. It is important to check everything. This is a situation that you will likely become responsible for and you need to go in with your eyes wide open.

Another option is for the bank to list a house for a while and then choose to change course after a certain number of days or may skip the standard listing and go directly to a real estate auction company. Several can be found online, each with their own bidding criteria. You may use a real estate broker, or go it alone. The bank does pay a commission to a buyer's agent. Be aware that the price advertised for the home is likely the opening bid, not the expected sales price, and most of these auction houses charge a buyer's fee of around 5%. Once the bank lists a home with an auction house, they will be charged an amount by that company. They will not pull a listing from an auction company. There is not a way around the system. If you do not like the system, do not play the game.

Unlike the courthouse auction earlier in the process, there will be a time for touring the home and getting a look at the floorplan and condition. Some prospective buyers bring an inspector or contractor in during this time because not all contracts allow for an inspection period, (depending on the auction company) and so they can have a solid estimate of costs of repairs so they know what they can feasibly pay for the home. There is a right to obtain traditional bank financing and to obtain the needed appraisal. You also do not have to deal with any right of redemption issues in this type of auction, as the bank has already taken possession and cleared the title. These auctions are usually well advertised in the community and may take place in the home or driveway or in something like a hotel conference room or real estate office. These homes are similar to a more traditional REO sale. You will have time to get a loan, and an inspector touring the home with you will help you understand what you may be getting into, but as the saying goes, expect the unexpected. There will be some unforeseen repair. Expect it. Budget for it. It will be expected that you have a significant earnest money deposit at the time of the auction, ready to go, if you are the winning bid.

Bidding has a funny way of affecting people. It has a tendency to bring out people's competitive side. Most people go in with an idea of what they want to pay, but too often I have seen bidding skyrocket out of control. I once attended an auction for a foreclosed home that had been listed for $417,000 on the market for months with no activity. The bank sent it to auction and I expected it to sell for around $375,000, a price that was supported by comparable sales in the area, compensating for the condition of the home. The opening bid was $250,000 and quickly rose to $350,000. At that point, those who were only there to get a steal of a deal started to slip away and it was down to two men, bidding against each other in quick succession. When it was over, one of them had agreed to pay $445,000 plus a 5% auction premium, for a home he could have bought three weeks before for $417,000. He paid more than the bank had been asking, which no one before that had been willing to pay. He got caught up in the process. It was one of the worst cases of auction fever I have ever personally witnessed. This man forgot some basic rules. Know your plan for the property, and know the maximum price you are willing to pay for it, based on sound estimates of repair costs and market value. It cannot be emotional, or you will end up losing in the long run.

Flipping

Having basic mathematical formulas can help both long term and short term investors ensure themselves from the volatility of the investment market. Flippers, whether it be in a financially distressed or physically distressed property, experience the highest rate of volatility, due to the expected and desired short term of the investment. Flippers are the day traders of the real estate market. It seems to be a quick in and out, but in reality an enormous amount of research is done before anything is purchased, at least by those who do it well. The potential of these short term investments to make money can be enormous, but is usually overstated and oversimplified in the media. There are as many good days as bad for most flippers or day traders. The myth that this money is quick and easy has cost a lot of people dearly over the years and many professionals, myself included, would caution that the reward does not justify the level of risk that is often assumed. Yet, even with all that caution, there will be some who are drawn to the process like a magnet. For those, I will review some basic guidelines to keep yourself on dry ground while you wait for your ship to come in.

The basic mathematical formula is simple. The maximum price you can pay for a house is the after repair value (ARV) x 70% - repair and soft costs. For example, if I have found a three bedroom, two bath home where the comparable sales values are $300,000 and the costs for repairs to get the home to the condition of those comparables is $18,000 and $30,000 in soft costs, then the formula would look like this:

$300,000 x 70% = $210000- $30,000= $180,000.

The most I can pay for that home and turn a profit is $180,000. If I pay more than that, I am putting myself at significant risk. If there is an unexpected or unbudgeted repair, which there nearly always is, or if the market softens in the time it takes you to make the repairs and turn the property, and the expected ARV drops, your profit margins will not be large enough to absorb those expenses and you will end up losing money. It is basic math.

Of course to use the math correctly, you must have accurate numbers. The AVR should be conservative, and determined by a local expert in neighborhood sales. If you are not that expert, you need to employ that expert, as it is the difference between large financial gain and large losses. The repair costs should be rounded up. If you are not a contractor, take your expected repair cost and double it. You have likely forgotten to estimate for a few things, and there will be things you haven't accounted for at all. Soft costs include items like the costs to sell the home after the flip, real estate fees, taxes, closing costs, loan fees. The list goes on and on. If you have miscalculated your soft costs, it can significantly impact your profit margin. Some might say that $180,000 for a house in a neighborhood of $300,000 houses is an embarrassingly low offer. It is. It ought to be. In fact this is the most you should possibly pay. $170,000 would be much better. If you can't or won't write the embarrassingly low offer, there is no money in it for you. Move on before it hurts you. The number one mistake made by short term real estate investors is paying too much for the property.

If you can write a respectably embarrassing offer, it is still important to remember that this will not be a process edited nicely to fit into a half hour TV show. Flipping takes weeks or months depending on how many people are doing the work. Unless you are a general contractor with a team working with you, or are planning on the expense of hiring a general contractor with a team, you will likely be investing months of time working to make the improvements to the property. Your time should be considered as part of the soft costs.

Several years ago, when low budget flips were common and demand was high, some potential buyers overlooked the mismatched hardware that a flipper got on clearance, or that the tiles were just a little off in every room. The house looked fresh and new, so maybe that bow in the floor or the cracks in the ceiling weren't a big deal. Someone would have noticed and repaired it if it was, right? Well, buyers have wised up on the whole. They go into flipped homes with a wary attitude about what is hiding under the shiny surface. They have heard the horror stories of flips done badly and "on the cheap".

You will not get anywhere near your ARV if you are using the bathroom vanity that doesn't really fit in the space, but was on special at the hardware box store. The buyer will notice that none of the appliances match because you went to the scratched and dented section and got whatever you could find.

My point is this: if you are going to flip as a serious way of making money, do it seriously. It is a job and must be done with that level of care and sophistication. Take the time and money to do it right. Be thorough. Have a plan and a firm budget. Be methodical about it, and it will pay off for you. If you are even more serious about doing it right and building wealth for yourself, you should also be considering how to manage your assets best and how to avoid certain tax liabilities. In my ideal flip scenario, I would buy a home cheap and in average condition in an improving neighborhood, one that would make sense as a single family rental where the rental income would cover my soft costs of holding the property. I would not make any major improvements to the home. It should be able to be rented in almost its existing condition. After using it as a rental for at least a year, when the property became vacant, I would then flip it if the market is right and take the profit, in a tax free

1031 exchange to a new flippable house. I will protect those profits from taxation and continue to expand my investment portfolio. If the market falters over the year, I can re-rent the home and wait for the market to heat up to flip the house.

Being able to sustain itself as a rental takes much risk out of the short term investment, because it can also be used in the long game of holding real estate to create wealth. There is no short term pressure. This kind of investment takes an eye for the market and a close watch for what you are looking for. It takes knowing the rental and sales markets as well as construction costs and appreciation predictions. There is nothing easy about it and it may not be quick money, but it is the smart play. Yes, you can make money in flipping, but you can also lose money. If you aren't prepared to lose sometimes, you aren't prepared to flip.

Home Seller's Guide

Chapter 8

Preparing to Sell

Sometimes the idea of selling your home creeps up on you. It starts as a small thought. Maybe you saw a home in the area of town you've always wanted to live come on the market and the idea of selling starts as almost a daydream. The new home daydream can be fun until it comes to the overwhelming idea of selling your existing home and that's where the daydream ends. But it doesn't have to be overwhelming and it doesn't have to end.

Sometimes selling is less of a daydream and more of a nightmare. Maybe it's a sudden shift of employment or family needs. The last thing you need in those circumstances is a panic about how to sell your home. Selling a home doesn't have to be panic inducing. What you need is information.

When I was in high school, I was not doing well in a class. My mother asked me if I had asked the teacher for help. I told her I hadn't; because honestly, I was too confused to even know what questions to ask. I've known plenty of home sellers who have experienced that same sense of dread. They don't want to reach out to a professional because they don't even know what they need to know. So, let's start with some basics.

What To Expect

Whether it's a daydream or a nightmare, it's important to know what the reality of the current housing market is for you. Is it a seller's market or a buyer's market, as we talked about earlier in this book? What is the average time a home like yours is taking to sell? And what is a good ballpark estimate for the sales price of your home? Any real estate broker truly familiar with the market can answer those basic questions off the top of their head, whether they are standing with you in the grocery store check-out line, or you are sitting across from them in their office. When you do what we do all day every day, those are things you know. The information will be broad and general, especially about a price for your home. That would depend greatly on area and condition and may not be something the real estate broker can pull from their memory banks. Or if your subdivision varies from the market as a whole, the information may not be accurate.

If you don't even know where to start to find a real estate professional, talk to family and friends. Look at neighborhood for sale signs, or search online. One of the early steps in all of this is to find the right real estate broker for you. What is right for someone else will not necessarily be right for you. Sometimes it is about personalities clicking, or not clicking, rather than a lack of knowledge or understanding of the market.

It seems that sometimes people do not know what should be expected from a real estate broker. All agents have their own strengths and weaknesses, but communication is always key. A good agent should be available to you. No, that does not mean they should return your call at 11pm on Friday night or 8am on a Sunday morning. We have lives and families and appreciate your respect in that matter. However, it does mean that they should return your call within a few hours if it is urgent, or at least within the business day for something more routine. Even if it is a quick text that says they got your message and are working on the issue you asked about, they should be available to you. A good agent should be willing to take the time to talk with you, without rushing you, to answer your questions without being put out. But all good agents are not the same, so it is important to understand what you want and don't want in a real estate broker.

There are some agents that have fantastic staff, but all too often sellers and buyers feel as if they have been bait and switched. An agent came into your home, told you what he was going to do to sell it, and then you never talk to him again. When you call, his secretary or a member of his "team" calls you back. This is not necessarily a bad thing in a well working team, but if you hired Bob because he was so friendly and relatable, then suddenly Bob disappears, it can be distressing. A mega agent is not necessarily the best agent in town, nor are they necessarily the right fit for you. There's nothing wrong with being a mega agent. But it does mean that not every property or client gets the attention they deserve from Bob personally. So, it is important for you to know what you want from a real estate professional.

Some agents will say "trust me" and that may be as much control as you want to have. Others will do what you ask and no more. If you enjoy micro-managing (and many people do) then that agent would work for you. I believe in educating my clients, so they have all the information they need to make the best decisions for themselves. Some agents are tech savvy; others will use a pencil and paper. Don't get caught up in technology at the expense of wisdom and experience, but it is important to acknowledge that a certain level of technology is a necessity for us to do our jobs well. Do you want a mega-agent? Do you want to always talk to the same person? What is important to you? Then reach out to an agent who meets those needs.

Reaching out to an agent can be as simple as a phone call or an email, and it should be fairly basic. Be sure to emphasize that you are in the early stages of the process and you are looking for information. This should keep real estate brokers from pressing you to sign a listing contract. They should not be shoving a contract down your throat, and if they are, please find a way to exit the situation. If you happen to miss them on the phone, or if you sent an email, be aware of how long it takes them to get back to you. If they do not return your phone call for days, realize that any potential buyers may get that same treatment. When you talk to the agent, tell them that you are looking for information about what to expect from your current housing market and how long homes are taking to sell. Then ask for a ballpark estimate of your home's worth. Good real estate brokers want to be a source of information.

You can help make that number more accurate by being prepared to share some basic information such as square footage, lot size and shape, details about your neighborhood, number of bedrooms and bathrooms and construction style. What year was the house built, and if the house is more than 15 years old, have there been any major updates or remodeling done? I usually ask people some questions that can catch them off guard. What was your favorite thing about the house when you bought it? And what one thing made you think twice about buying it? Some homeowners find these questions odd, but the truth is, what drew you to a home will likely catch the next buyer's eye as well, and whatever drew you away will likely do the same and can have a big impact on the home's value.

Some brokers may give you simple answers. The best brokers will want to help educate you and give you more specific details about what you can do to prepare without a lot of pressure to sign sign sign. To get the best feel for your home, they will need to set foot inside. This is what I call a pre-listing appointment.

A pre-listing appointment is usually a brief home visit where I can walk through the home and see the condition of the property, so I can come up with the best price. It is also a good time to talk about your goals and timelines. Sometimes small upgrades or changes can make a big difference in selling a home. I can point those things out to a potential seller so they can make the most of their home's profits. I will also ask for how much you owe on the home, enabling me to have an accurate estimate of how much money you can expect to make off the sale of your home after paying all the fees and costs associated with selling a home.

I have never walked into an appointment in someone's home with the intention to be rude, but being less than honest with you will do nothing to sell your home. Have you ever seen those shows on cable TV where they hide cameras in the open house, and people walk through and say what they *really* think of a property? Are people really that brutal in real life? Yes, they are. And sometimes an honest conversation up front can save you a lot of heart ache. One of my former bosses had a poster in his office of a lovable looking dog that read, *If I can smell it, I can't sell it!* Harsh, but true. The odors we live with in our home day to day have a way of becoming undetectable to us. We literally become "nose blind." The nicks and scratches in the doorways, the fingerprints on the sliding door, our eye becomes immune to them. It doesn't mean you are a bad housekeeper. It certainly doesn't mean you are a bad person, but if $300 of new carpet is the difference between selling your home in 10 days, or having it on the market for 6 months and selling for $10,000 less, I am going to tell you that it would sell better with new carpet in Fido's room. Please don't feel judged.

My job is to make the most of your home within your budget and timeline. There are lots of handy tricks and tips I have picked up along the way from contractors and home stagers to make homes feel bigger, brighter, cleaner and newer. I can help you find the source of an odor and nip it in the bud. I can show you that the lighting sconces on the front of the home don't match or are crooked and by straightening them or spending $30 on matching ones, your home looks cleaner. On a recent listing I noticed that the front of their home looked a little flat and plain, especially in comparison to some neighboring homes. After taking a minute to decide what it was about the neighboring homes that made them look sharper, I realized my seller's home was lacking the shutters around the windows that their neighbors had. I asked if they had ever considered getting shutters, that it would really make the front of the home pop, especially in photographs. I saw the wife shoot a look at her husband. He admitted that she had wanted shutters for years, but he hadn't bothered. For less than $100 they purchased shutters and painted them to match their contrast color. It looked like a brand new home in front. And yet most people couldn't tell what they had done. Landscaping work? One person asked if they had redone all their siding. No! It was just some shutters. Bringing someone into your home that isn't blind to the sights and smells can be invaluable. Try to keep your feelings from getting hurt and understand that what you are being told is to help you.

In the pre-listing appointment, I will typically leave an information packet about home pricing, and the current market conditions, as well as a copy of the listing contract for you to look over at your convenience. If there is time, I might go over the broad points of the contract and other forms to help you know what to expect when you are actually ready to move forward. I never want anyone to sign something that they are not comfortable with or do not understand. If you don't understand something that is put in front of you, don't hesitate to take some extra time to go over it and make sure that all parties are on the same page.

When you are ready to move forward, there should be another meeting. At this point, the real estate broker should have an exact idea of what listing price they would recommend for your home. They should be able to show you a marketing strategy as well as an estimate of the proceeds from the sale.

Chapter 9

Pricing, Marketing and Staging your Home

Pricing Your Home

Pricing a home can be tricky. We have to take into account that we must be prepared to sell the home twice: once to the buyer and once to the lender in the form of an appraisal. You may price your home $10,000 higher than any other home in the neighborhood. You may even find a buyer willing to pay that, but if the comparable homes that have recently sold do not justify that price, the home will not appraise at the needed value and the deal will likely fall apart well into the process. A listing price must be shown to be valid by comparing it to other similar homes in the area.

If you happen to live in a community of identical homes, built at the same time with the same building materials and several of those homes have sold in the last few months, pricing your home will be a snap. The only variables will be how well the home has been maintained and perhaps location within the development. If you live in a less cookie cutter area, pricing a home correctly is a process. An accurate value is best determined by multiple pricing techniques. Most frequently those are a micro-market average, a macro- market average, and a price per square foot. How each of those is weighted within the equation will depend on each individual property.

As I review these numbers with homeowners, I often hear them talk about why their homes should be priced for more. Sometimes this is their heart value- how much they love their home and all the wonderful memories made there. Some want to take what they paid for their home plus every dollar and hour of work they have ever put into maintaining it and improving it and use that as a value. Sometimes they use words like unique, special and different; therefore it is worth more. It is understandable to be attached to your home. I know I am attached to mine. But it is important to take a step back and realize that while your heart value might be one thing, the market value may be something totally different and that in no way diminishes the love and memories that were made and shared within those walls. It is important to remember that value is not a static equation like adding 2 + 4. There are other outside factors in the economy that play a huge part in determining your home's value. And most of all, it is important to remember that what is special to one, may make no difference to another, or worse, be seen as something unattractive. For instance, the pond in your back yard that you love to look at every morning while you sip your coffee, which brings you so much peace and serenity to start your day may be seen as a huge drowning hazard for the family with small children. Or the contemporary light fixtures that you think make your home feel sleek and modern, others might find cold and unappealing. The wheelchair accessible bathroom may have been a must for your wheelchair bound family member, but may make no difference to someone else and the wheelchair ramp to the front door may be seen as a flaw rather than an indispensable form of access.

So, how do you know if the pond adds value, or if your customized fixtures should stay or go? A good rule of thumb is the 50/50 rule. If you were to take all the potential home buyers for your home specifically, that would be 100% of your potential buying pool. If more than half of those people would likely find the attribute to be a positive selling feature, then it justifies raising the home's value. If it is less than 50%, it does not. If it is likely that less than 30% of potential buyers would find it to be a positive feature, it will likely cause a drop in home value. Some items may be easy for you to remove or replace, some are less changeable, like a pond in the yard or a swimming pool. Depending on where you are in the country a swimming pool can be a great asset, where in other areas it is seen as a time eater and extra expense that can only be used a few months of the year. Determining how others will see your home depends on a great deal of geographical data such as census reports and school demographics. It can give you an idea of what your potential likely buyers will look like. A real estate professional can help you determine what attributes of your home are assets and what might have been an asset to you, but a detriment to others.

Each home is individual. Be wary of a real estate broker who only uses one price method to justify their projected list price for your home. Many times I have had one method indicate a certain price range while the other two show me a completely different number. Usually, they overlap in a certain range and that is statistically the best price for your home. If a price per square foot is showing $325,000, while the macro and micro price are showing a range of $250,000 to $275,000 that shows me that putting too much emphasis on the price per square foot would take it out of sync with the market as a whole. There must be a balance. But if I only used one pricing technique, I run the risk of overpricing a property beyond what it would ever appraise or sell for, leaving the home languishing on the market while homes around it sell even faster than before, since they are now seen as more of a bargain over your own home.

Be wary of real estate brokers who urge you to list your home above the average. If you interview Agents A, B, and C and A and C both show you that the market says your home is worth between $250,000 and $260,000 and Agent B says he wants to list it for $275,000, your antenna should go up, warning you that there is a problem. Everyone wants to sell their home for as much money as possible and the pull of those higher numbers can be hard to fight. Usually those same agents are the most dynamic. They may have a very high tech sales pitch that leaves you feeling wowed. But it may be the last "wow" moment you have in the process.

I would love to tell you that all real estate brokers are created equal, that we all have the best of intentions and put your needs before our own, but too often I have seen that to not be the case. Too many real estate brokers are willing to "buy the listing", to puff up the price to make sure they get your business. They know the home won't sell for the number they have suggested, but now you are in a contract, and they figure after a reasonable amount of time, they can talk you into lowering the price in response to the showing feedback. Sadly, now you are listed at $260,000 just as Agent A suggested, but you have wasted a month or two on the market. And the longer the home is on the market, the less power you have as a seller in the negotiation process. Why would agents do this? Unfortunately, our system is set up in a way that encourages this practice. People want to hear that their home is worth more money. It makes it more likely that you as the seller will sign a contract with the terms the agent wants, like a longer listing or a higher commission.

It also provides a great deal of advertising for the agent. When you drive through town and see sign after sign for a particular agent in people's yards, you tend to think how successful and well regarded they must be. So, when you need to sell your home, you take the name and number and ask them to sell your home. It is the cheapest form of advertising an agent has.

When I see a sign in a yard for more than the standard market time, my opinion of the agent drops. They clearly have not priced the property properly and have not served their clients best interests. That doesn't mean that you should never have to lower your price if your agent has done their job. There is always a range of acceptable price options. If you chose to start at the highest price possible, you may still need to lower your price to renew interest in the property, but a good agent will have forewarned you to that option. Fight the instinct to be wowed by a high price in a listing presentation. Follow the path towards knowledge of the market and open information.

Educate yourself to look beyond the simple sales prices in the comparable homes to also evaluate sales price vs. list price vs. original list price. If a home was on the market for 75 days at $250,000, then lowered the list price to $230,000 and was sale pending 15 days later, and sold 35 days later for $222,000, what was the true value of that home? What was the correct list price? As an experienced real estate broker, that shows me the home was listed too high originally. Either the agent bought the listing or the sellers were unwilling to listen to their broker's advice and insisted on listing the home for more than it was worth. If the original list price had been $230,000, it likely would have only been on the market for 10-20 days and would have likely sold for more than $222,000. And don't be afraid to ask hard questions of the agents you are interviewing. If Agent B is so sure he can sell your home for significantly more money than Agents A or C, ask him how he came to that price. Make sure it is using more than one pricing technique and ask him about his most recent sold home's sales price vs. list price vs. original list price.

The agent should always be showing you the list price vs. sales price on all the comparable homes to help you establish what you should expect for yourself. They should provide you with an estimate of the amount of proceeds from the sale of the home. This number should be based off of a projected sales price, rather than a list price. If homes in the area are selling for 97% of their list price, (preferably their original list price) then it would be safe to take 97% of your list price and establish that as your projected sales price. From there, a Net Sheet, or Estimated Proceeds from Sale worksheet should break down the costs associated with selling the home. If your projected sales price was $220,000, you would then subtract these costs, including the outstanding balance on your current mortgage, taxes, title fees, and your real estate broker's commission, from that amount and have a rough idea of how much money you will receive at the end of the sale. Your real estate broker should talk to you about current market conditions and other fees that may be customary in your area or in the current market, such as inspections and surveys and perhaps giving a credit to the buyer to help cover some or all of their closing costs. That will vary greatly based on the current market. Some fees will vary slightly. The payoff amount for your current loan is a set amount, but will change depending on the exact date the home closes and the loan is paid in full. Taxes will be prorated to the sale date to split the cost between the buyer and seller for the appropriate amount of days that each party owned the property. Title and escrow fees will vary depending on your choice of companies, as will real estate broker's commissions.

There is no such thing as a "standard commission" amongst real estate brokerages. That would be a violation of the law. However, there are likely norms for your area. The key is to get what you pay for. There are likely discount brokerages in your area. They may charge a flat fee or a low commission, but you need to be realistic about what that fee provides. Usually it is a contract and a listing on the MLS with pictures you provide. Often they never set foot in the home or help you prepare for the process in any way, not even helping you determine your home's value. It is basically a form of advertising for those interested in selling their home on their own.

There will be agents willing to charge 5% or 5.5%, or maybe 6% and some will ask for 7%. The question is, what are you getting for 7% of the sales price of your home that you are not getting for 5.5%? It is a fair question. Don't be afraid to ask it. There are services provided that can justify a higher commission rate, even a proven track record of performance may justify the extra pay, but if the answer is "that is what I charge" with no added service or benefit to you, there is no reason to choose that agent over another.

Marketing Your Home

The last needed element in a listing presentation is a marketing plan. A marketing plan is not some vague PowerPoint presentation about how many homes their brokerage has sold. It is a day by day, week by week, proven strategy to get traffic into your home and get a written offer. The first step in this plan would involve preparing the home, fixing little things to get it ready as was discussed in the pre-listing appointment. The next would be pictures.

High quality professional listing pictures are not an optional part of the process anymore. Gone are the days of an agent walking through a home with a camera or even a cell phone, snapping a few somewhat blurry shots and being on their way. No. I recently met some sellers at their home with my photographer. After an hour, my seller turned to me and said, "This is nothing like I thought it would be. I thought you'd come through for a few minutes and be gone. This is a lot of work!" Yes, it is. Because it is the most important, most visible advertising I will provide. In 2012 over 90% of home buyers were viewing homes online and that number continues to rise. And now more than 55% are viewing homes on a mobile devise (The National Association of Realtors and Google, 2015). In that information rich environment, buyers expect to see pictures that accurately represent the home. However the same study suggests that the average dwell time on a particular opening image is less than 8 seconds before the buyer either clicks to see more or moves on to another home. 8 seconds; that is how long I have to capture a potential buyer's attention and draw them to your home, wherever the ad might be.

In the old days, we set up virtual tours to take buyers through the layout of the home, so they could picture the home's floorplan easily. That is no longer the case. Effective online marketing of images starts with an outside view and proceeds to the 5 most appealing features of the home, no matter where they are located. If the buyer makes it past the 5th image, they will overwhelmingly look at the remaining images. If the first five images are unappealing, buyers will move on to another home. It is a difficult question. Can you sell your home in 8 seconds? I have to, and pictures are key to that process.

Along with fantastic pictures that accurately represent the home, an engaging writing style and valuable information about the home are also critical in any web advertisements. Along with a dedicated website for your home, it should also be linked to social media, and IDX websites like Zillow to get the widest possible distribution. The advertising model for each home will vary, but there should be a laid out plan. Week 1 we will do these three things. Week 2 we will add these activities. Week 3 these advertisements will be in place. Week 4 we will look at all collected data, discuss activity and price point and make a new strategy. Weekly or bi-monthly reports should be given to you to show where leads are originating, what marketing is being effective and where potential interest is located.

There are some myths about marketing that should be expelled. Let's talk open houses. First of all, open houses should fall into the 'market the agent rather than the home' category, because they are and always have been about capturing unrepresented buyers. But it is a dying practice. It is not necessary in most markets. Add it to the list of things that websites have replaced, rather like the volume of encyclopedias in your grandparent's house. According to the National Association of Realtors, in 2014 only 9% of home buyers found their home at an open house. That is down from 16% in 2004 (National

Association of Realtors, 2015). That means in 2004, your chances of selling your home, after cleaning it and leaving for hours on end, was abysmal. Now, it's practically hopeless and quite frankly, not worth the time and energy sellers have to put in to prepare the home.

As there are things to be wary of in pricing your home, be wary of some marketing that goes hand in hand with the earlier problem. Why would an agent want a home on the market for a day longer than it needs to be? Don't they want to sell it fast? Selling it fast may not be their first priority. The longer the sign sits in the yard, the more self-promotion they receive off the sign as well as mailers that may be distributed to the surrounding neighborhood. Are those flyers and postcards designed to help sell your home? No, they aren't. They are designed to market the agent themselves and draw in more listings. If those sorts of activities are appearing on a weekly marketing plan, be aware of their real priority. They aren't a bad thing. It may help sell your home, but the odds are low. Another similar marketing strategy may be an ad in the local home magazine. You may see them at the grocery stores or in the doctor's office waiting rooms. They look pretty sleek and fancy and there is absolutely nothing wrong with your home being listed in one. But be aware of the real purpose. These magazines are typically published once a month, and therefore in most markets the homes aren't even available by the time the magazines hit the stand.

So, why would we, as agents, waste our money? Because it's not about the home, it's about us. We want the phone to ring. It doesn't matter that the house they are calling about sold two weeks before. It's a new client and new income for us. But, in order to place an ad with great looking houses in it that make people call us, we have to have listings that stay on the market long enough to place the ad. So, do we mind overpricing your home for a month? No. It is a great advertising tool for us. But it is not good for you. So, when you look at a marketing plan, make sure it is geared to benefit you and your home, rather than the agent representing you. Be aware of words like "included in my ad" or "part of my advertising" or "featured on my". Basically any "me" or "my" words, mean that ad is to promote them, and your house can tag along for the ride. It's not bad to tag along, but it won't do you much good. It's not even meant to.

Preparing Your Home

Hiring a real estate professional cannot relieve you of all the responsibility of preparing your home. A property must be prepped. Everything your mother every told you about first impressions is doubly true about a house's debut on the market. Take an extra few days and do it right. Before listing is the time to fix the small dings in the doorways, to deep clean the home, and make it picture perfect. This is also the time to remove the clutter. Take down personal pictures. Pull the kids artwork off the fridge. Replace dimming light bulbs. Get rid of wiring from electronics that may be dangling about. Empty seasonal items not in use from the closets. The goal is to make the home appear as open and bright as possible. Sometimes this means moving some furniture around, or moving some pieces out of the house altogether. If it is practical in your price range, your real estate broker may have a home stager come in and optimize the look and feel of the home. It is also the time to neutralize your home. Paint over bold colors with something natural and neutral, though white is not usually the best option. Also, eliminate too many patterns which have a way of shrinking the space to a buyer's eye.

It can be hard to de-personalize your home, to take down photos of your family, or personal items that may add to the clutter, but the whole point is to not have someone think of this space as yours, and rather see it as a place they could live. Anything you can do to make it more comfortable for them to be in the space is helpful, things like not having used towels in the bathroom or being able to see dirty cloths.

When staging a home, the key is to sell an idea, a lifestyle. We may place a small table on a back patio, so people can picture themselves drinking their coffee there in the morning while reading the paper. Realistically, if they don't read the paper now, there is no reason to believe that moving to a different home would suddenly encourage them to start doing that, but there isn't much logic to how people feel in a home. A throw on the couch makes them feel like it is a warm and happy place to be with their family. Plants make it feel alive and airy. We don't want anything seen that can destroy that illusion of what life will be like in the home- things like laundry hampers and trash cans. Of course, when they live there, they will have dirty clothes and trash, but no one wants to picture that as part of their new life, so put the trash cans out of site. Make sure laundry is put away.

It is a real pain to live in a home that is for sale, to have it ready to sell the illusion at a moment's notice. Every real estate agent understands, but it is what needs to be done and it will be worth it to have great showings.

Life happens. The home will not stay in a perpetual state of cleanliness, but when the house is being shown, it will be important to straighten up and get it in "showing" condition. No dirty dishes in the sink. Take the trash out. Clean up the scattered toys from children. Empty the cat litter, or anything else that might cause an unpleasant odor. But also avoid air fresheners or scented candles. The adage to bake bread to help lure in buyers is more trouble than it is worth. It would be better to not have any dishes in the sink. Cozy smells are nice, but do not make them artificially. An overabundance of smelly candles do not add ambiance. It makes people think your home smells and you are covering up the stench. If you want to add a fresh scent, you may consider tucking a single fabric softener sheet in a drawer in the bathroom, or a box of baking soda in the fridge. (Yes, they will open your fridge). These absorb odor and have a natural, more neutral scent. Music in the background of a showing can be very effective, but make sure it is the right music. Some agents may have a playlist you can access to play before you leave. Anything vocal should be off the list immediately. Light instrumental is usually best. I have a Pandora station I suggest for my sellers.

You will also need to secure your personal items. The most common items stolen from homes in open houses or showings are jewelry and prescription drugs. Either lock them up, tuck them way out of sight, or take them with you. It is not that other real estate agents or even yours would knowingly let people steal from you, but you are inviting strangers into your home. You need strangers to come into your most intimate spaces. So, protect yourself. Most importantly, you need to leave the property during the showings. No matter how inconvenient it is, you, your family and pets must go if you truly want all your work to pay off.

Real Estate Seasons

People believe that real estate is a seasonal cycle. People widely expect the best time to sell a home to be in the summer months. It is certainly true that a good deal of volume is done in the summer, but if you find yourself ready to make a move in November, do not despair. National sales statistics show that fall and winter selling is not doomed. In fact, most sellers are surprised to find that statistically the shortest time on the market by month is December and the month you are most likely to receive a full price offer is February (The National Association of Realtors, 2016). So, why does winter get such a bad real estate reputation? The same home in the summer might be shown a dozen times, and in December it may only be shown once. It may feel like a fruitless effort, but the truth is that while the number of buyers decreases in the winter, the buyers who are left are serious about buying a home. Let's face it, no one bundles up in a coat and gloves and trudges out in the cold if they aren't serious about buying a home. And because so many sellers don't want to deal with muddy foot prints and holiday decorations, fewer homes are on the market. So while your home might have been only one in ten a buyer was choosing from in August, it may be the absolute jewel of the market in January. Every season has advantages and disadvantages. Season should rarely determine when to list your home over the many other deciding factors in your lives.

Chapter 10

The Selling Process

The Offer

Once the showings and home preparation is over, there is still the matter of actually selling your home. At some point, you will receive an offer on your home. If you are lucky, you will be in a market where you may receive more than one. Multiple offers are a beautiful thing. What a powerful feeling to know you have more than one interested buyer. But don't let it go to your head so much that you start trying to push buyers for more. I have seen it play out again and again. It's as if sellers get drunk with power and start making very bad choices. They will counter offer a good, solid offer over a few silly items. After a back and forth, a frustrated buyer feels pushed too far and walks away, and the remaining buyers have moved on to other houses. What a way to make a disaster of a perfectly lovely scenario.

     If multiple offers are likely, they are likely to come in the first week. Sometimes sellers who get multiple offers in the first few days turn to their real estate agent and say "why didn't we list the house for more?" thinking, clearly, if many were interested at this price, at least a few would have paid even more. That is simply not true. If you want to know the highest and best price you can really get from your home, multiple offers are the best way to do that. The Pricing pyramid shows us that a higher price point means less interest.

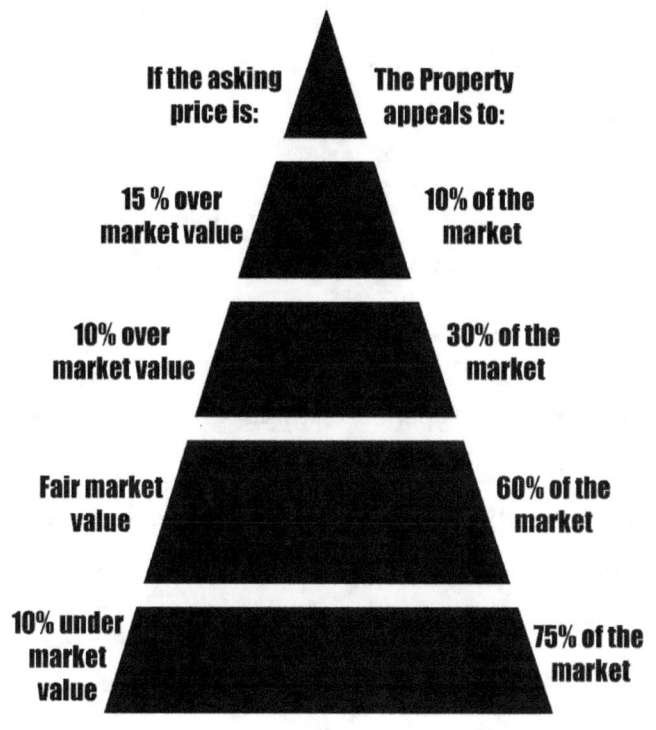

Another comment real estate brokers here when properties receive offers quickly is "what are we paying *you* for?" as if throwing a sign in the yard is not worthy of a significant commission. Please be aware that a real estate broker's work did not begin with a yard sign and does not end when an offer is received. In fact, their work is likely just getting started. A good real estate broker will be there through every step of the closing process to make sure every element of the process is handled smoothly. And selling a home involves many steps.

The offer is sometimes a confusing thing. Some sellers get caught up on the idea that another offer might come in. Maybe it will. But there is an expression; *a bird in the hand is worth two in the bush.* The offer you have on paper is infinitely superior to any lagging, dragging verbal interest. When people are truly interested, they write offers. It doesn't take a lot of time. You should not be waiting around for days for an offer you heard was maybe coming. Take written offers seriously. The rest is just hot air.

When reading an offer, don't get overly fixated on the price. The price is certainly important, but there are other areas to watch out for, such as:

- How much earnest money are they depositing?
- What kind of financing are the buyers using? Is that financing compatible with your home and area? FHA and USDA have strict standards about a home's condition that your home may or may not meet. How secure is their financing? Are the

buyer's pre-approved for a mortgage loan for the amount that they have offered to pay?

- What other items are the buyers asking you to pay for? How are the title fees being divided? What about a survey or home warranty? Are they asking for concessions for items like closing costs or repairs?
- Is their purchase contingent on the sale of another property?
- How long will they take to close on the sale?

All of these items can have an impact on the sale of your home and you should be aware of all of them.

You have only three options when presented with an offer. You can accept it as it is written with no changes, you can reject it entirely or you may counter offer. The counter offer is where people get confused. To be perfectly clear, a counter offer is a rejection. You cannot change an item or two and then accept the offer. That is not legal. When you counter offer, you are rejecting their offer unless they accept certain changes you have made. Then the contract goes back to the buyers and they have the same three options; to accept your counter offer, reject your counter offer or counter your counter offer. This can go back and forth indefinitely. It might be price or closing date or other terms that cause the disagreement. Negotiation is not a bad thing but it can be taken too far. It is important to remember that this stage of negotiations is one of three possible windows. If you negotiate too aggressively at this stage, you risk causing problems later on.

The Closing Process

Once the contract had been agreed upon, the escrow process will begin to move forward. This is the time where both the buyer and the seller do everything they are required to do to fulfil the contract and sell the property. An average escrow period will last around 30-45 days. At first it will seem like a lot of things are happening. The buyers will deposit earnest money with either your real estate brokerage or the title office to be held until the close of sale. This is to show their good faith intent to buy the home. This should be in the first 2 business days.

A whole home inspection will be ordered by the buyers, usually to be completed in the first 10-15 days after acceptance of a signed contract. You will need to make sure all the utilities are functioning for this, and you will need to leave the home for several hours while the inspector works. You will want your home to be in showing condition for the inspection.

Even if your home is in great shape, no home is perfect. The inspector will find something wrong, maybe a whole list of somethings, and they may seem like knit picky items. Try not to let it get to you. It is just part of the process and the less emotional you are about it, the easier it will be for you in the long run. Once the buyers receive their report, they can ask for any items listed to be repaired. You cannot demand to see a copy of the report. It is something purchased by the buyer and only the buyer has a right to it. They may opt to give it to you, but they may not. But if they ask for repairs, you do have the right to ask for those specific portions of the report. This is the second window for negotiation. If the buyer asks for 8 items to be repaired, you may accept the written addendum, or reject it and refuse to make any repairs, or you may write a counter offer saying you will fix some and not others. If you have pushed them to the very last penny negotiating a purchase price, this phase will be more difficult. No one wants to feel taken advantage of.

In extreme cases, the buyer may find the condition of the home to be vastly different than what they thought they were buying when they wrote the offer. In that case, they have the right to reject the home based on its condition and thereby terminate the offer, and receiving a refund of their earnest money. It is usually something drastic. The roof is not stable. The foundation is crumbling. It should be a major thing, though some buyers will try to use any small item to get out of a sale that they may have just gotten cold feet about. It is certainly disappointing to have a sale fall through, but sometimes the best thing to do is simply move on. Moving on quickly gets them their earnest money back and allows you to re-list your home for sale for the next buyer. No one wants this to happen, but when it does there's no point in getting bogged down by it. If a major issue is brought up, it's time to decide what you want to do. It is likely that the next buyer will react similarly. It may be necessary to make the repair, or disclose the issue and lower the price to compensate for the issue. This may limit the potential buyer's ability to finance the home purchase. Repairs are common in any home. It is the size and expense of repair that will vary.

Once you have agreed upon repairs, the next step is an appraisal. An appraisal is ordered by the buyer's lending institution. The appraiser looks at recently sold homes in the area and decides what your home is worth. The lender will not loan more than what the home is worth. If a home comes in under value it can make the whole sale fall apart. Once again, you will need to leave the home while the appraiser comes in, though it won't be for as long. The appraiser will only look at major systems of the home. It may be a week later, but the appraisal will return a value and an appraisal report. If the value is equal or more than the purchase price, the sale moves forward. If the appraisal comes back under value, our third window of negotiations opens. The bigger the price shortfall, the more likely this is to become an unsurmountable obstacle. If it is only off by a few $1000, there are likely compromises that can be made. If the appraisal did not consider valid characteristics of the home, the lender can challenge the appraisal and send in a written report asking for these issues to be addressed, but I have never had a challenged appraisal come in at full value. Closer, perhaps, but not full value. If a real estate broker priced your home correctly, the odds of an appraisal problem are slim, but in areas where the market is quickly appreciating, it can and does come up.

The appraiser also has the power to make a repair a condition of financing. These can be fairly major repairs such as putting on a new roof, or something as small as having a furnace serviced. Once a repair is listed on an appraisal report, negotiation is over. If you want to sell your home to that buyer, you will need to make that repair. If the buyer is using an FHA loan, that appraisal is tied to your property for any FHA buyer for the next 90-120 days, meaning if you don't make the repair, you will not be able to sell it to any FHA buyer. It is usually a case of make the repair or let the sale fail. At this point, the home has likely been off the market for two to three weeks. If there is a way for you to make the repair, the best course of action is almost always to do it.

Once the appraisal is in, and repairs have been made, things with the sale will seem to fall quiet. It is likely an illusion because there are professionals working behind the scenes to keep things running smoothly, a real estate broker, a title officer, a loan officer, all working to get all the paperwork where it needs to be on time. With any luck, it will work like a well-oiled machine, but even the best maintained machines have a glitch every now and again. Sometimes loan documents are delayed because more documentation is needed, or there is a backlog of property files waiting for lending approval. Don't panic, but be forewarned. Sometimes a closing date is fluid. Be ready to roll with changing days and times. It is simply part of the process.

This lull of activity, or perceived lull, is the perfect time to focus on the actual moving process, packing boxes and making moving arrangements. While packing, keep an eye out for things that belong with the home; spare keys, garage door openers, and appliance manuals. Find an empty drawer to leave those items in. You will not need them, and it is considered polite. And who doesn't want to be a well-mannered seller? Also listed in the good manners selling tips is to leave the home clean. The deep clean from the listing is hopefully still keeping it shining, but moving is a messy process. Make sure to give yourself time to sweep, and vacuum one last time on your way out. A little note left behind telling the new homeowners when trash day is and maybe which mailbox is theirs if you have a group of mailboxes also never hurt anyone. Just think about those things that you would want as a buyer and try to do the same for someone else.

It's simply called being a nice person. Even when all of the negotiations and addendums and legal forms are signed, being a nice person is basically free and will leave you feeling good about the transaction.

Typically the day before closing, or even the morning of, the buyer will come through the house one last time for a final walk through. The purpose of this is to make sure the roof hasn't caved in, and that most commonly, all the things that should be there, are, and things that ought not to be are not. No one wants to move in to find you left a junky couch in the basement. They also don't want to arrive to find missing light fixtures of bathroom mirrors. Sometimes it is tricky for a seller to know what they can take from a home and what they can't. The legal terms are personal property vs. fixtures. A home's fixtures include light fixtures, built in shelving and ceiling fans. Those may seem obvious, but things like bathroom mirrors can be a little trickier. If there is any ambiguity, and something is important to you, try to think ahead and be sure to itemize it in the sales contract with a statement like *front porch swing not included in the sale*. Porch swings would typically be personal property, as would items like above ground hot tubs and potted plants. But in ground hot tubs and plants that are in the ground would be fixtures and included in the sale, unless specifically excluded when the contract was written. Blinds are fixtures. Curtains are personal property. Does it seem complicated? It is. So here are my two rules of thumb. First- err on the side of caution and second- when in doubt, ask your real estate professional. I usually tell my clients if they need a tool to remove it from their wall, they need to talk to me about it first. Items like pictures that you can lift and remove from the wall are pretty easy to classify, but what about the free standing shelf anchored to the wall? Or curtain rods? It is worth asking about; because nothing is worse than a dispute about a mirror you already packed during a final walk through.

Once the loan documents have arrived at the title office and the final walk through is done, you will meet at the title office to sign papers. This is called the signing appointment. Please make sure you have a valid ID, and either have your social security card, or know your number. The stack of papers won't be as long as the buyers, but it will be extensive. There are three steps to a home closing; signing, funding and recording. Signing happens when the pen meets the paper. Funding is when the loan is funded, all the money switches hands and recording is when the sale is recorded with the county. They all have to happen and in that order in order for the sale to be complete. In some areas signing and funding will happen together and you will leave your signing appointment with a check for the proceeds from the sale of your home. Sometimes the funds will be wire transferred to either your bank account or to another title office handling the purchase of your new home. Then keys are exchanged and you take a deep breath because you have survived one of the biggest stresses of adulthood. You have sold a home. The only worry left is whether you now owe more money on your taxes because you made money selling your house. For most, the answer is no. The current 2017 tax code states that proceeds from the sale of a personal property are exempt for capital gains tax up to $250,000 for a single tax payer or $500,000 for a married couple filing jointly. This is only for your "main home". If the term "main home" seems vague to you, you are not alone. It is accepted that your main home is a home you have owned and used as your main residence for two of the last five years. That means if you owned the home for five years, and lived in it for three of those years, but moved out two years ago and have been renting it out, you would still be eligible for this tax exemption. If it is an investment property that you have not lived in or owned less than two years, you would need to pay capital gains tax on the proceeds of the sale or use a 1031 exchange for investment properties.

Understanding The Process

Selling real estate is not as easy as sticking a for sale sign in your yard. Even if an offer comes quickly there are hours of work to get the project to its conclusion. Some of the stress of managing a sale can be reduced by using the right professional to keep things moving in the right direction, by being prepared for the small changes and delays, and for understanding that the process is not a personal judgement on you, or your family. It is hard to take something as personal as a home and make it a business transaction, but that emotional separation from the home will make the process easier for you to navigate.

Chapter 11
For Sale By Owner

There are agents who hate those "for sale by owner" types. I have heard them say, "Would they try to do heart surgery on themselves?" It's an attitude I've never understood. One thing about my job that I have always appreciated, especially with a special needs daughter whose health can be so precarious, is that no matter how important property may feel to someone, no lives actually hang in the balance.

I believe that my expertise is valuable and important, that the transaction is more likely to go smoothly and you are more likely to walk away with what you want if I am there to help you. Still, I will concede that selling a home is not open heart surgery and most people can do it on their own with the right knowledge and the time and willingness to properly engage in the process.

Sellers want to avoid using a real estate broker for a variety of reasons. Often they want to avoid pushy sales people who they feel are taking advantage of them. I have had enough run-ins with bad agents to understand that emotion. There is a reason that real estate brokers rank somewhere near used car salesmen in levels of trust in national surveys. You should not feel pressured by someone who works for you. You should not be confused by the process or what is going on. When you hire someone to work for you, their job should be to orient and prepare you for the process. If agents are pressuring clients, leaving them confused, I can't blame anyone for wanting to go it alone.

Other sellers are what I have come to know as the "control enthusiast". These are sellers who want to be in control of every aspect of the transaction and prefer to maintain some of that control by selling the home on their own. I empathize. I have a fair amount of enthusiasm for control myself. But in a good agent relationship, you should not feel any loss of control. It simply becomes a team effort. You have the ultimate say in the list and sales price of the home that you are willing to accept. You have control over acceptable showing times and how those are scheduled. You should have control over how much feedback from buyers you receive and how often that information is presented to you. There isn't anything wrong with going it alone and maintaining control. All I can say is that there is a way to maintain the control without carrying the entire burden, but it will be key to find the right agent who you can work with to make that happen.

Some sellers want to save the money that would be spent on agents' representation. With sales commissions somewhere around 6% of the sales price, that is 6% most sellers wish they could keep for themselves. Can a seller list their home for less? Usually. There are usually discount brokerages that will put the home on the local MLS for a flat fee. Or a seller can list it themselves, and while it will cost less up front, it will not be free. Signs will need to be purchased, attorney's fees or pre-written documents will need to be purchased, title fees, surveys, advertising, but most of all, it will cost the seller time. There will be time to research comparable property sales to reach a fair sales price, time to research and collect homeowner's association documents, and obtaining legal descriptions of the home and lot. As a seller, you will be responsible for obtaining all the proper disclosures for your home that are required by the Federal and State governments, and these will vary depending on the age and location of your home.

Having a 'For Sale By Owner' home also attracts a certain type of buyer. Sometimes they are equally wary of real estate professionals, but more often than not, they think it will save them money. If the seller is trying to save 6%, the buyer cannot also save that same money. So they question is, who is really saving money?

There is a right way of going about listing your home for sale by owner and a way not to. Like it or not, many buyers want and like having an agent by their side. So the first decision you must make when choosing to go it alone **is whether or not you are** willing to work with a buyer's agent, followed immediately by how much will you pay them? If you are not willing to work with any agent, you must understand that you are eliminating a group of eligible buyers.

There are a couple of hard and fast "thou shalt not" rules that you should always keep in mind. "Thou shalt not" call a bunch of agents and ask them to come give you an analysis of the current value of your home only to take that number and list it yourself. Even worse, do not call a friend who is a real estate broker and ask for their free advice so you can list it yourself. It is rude. There is nothing wrong with asking someone's opinion, but when you have no intention to use their services, it is taking advantage of people, people who don't get paid unless they sell a home. You may need some of these agents to help you find the right buyer. Do not alienate them. If you don't feel capable of finding the information to come up with a fair list price on your own, without asking agents to find comparable properties for you, you don't have the skills that will be necessary to successfully sell your own home.

"Thou shalt not" walk through your home and snap pictures of each room on your cell phone and upload them onto the web with a sentence or two about your home and expect it to sell. You will be in competition with every other home on the market, especially those with professional photos and staging, and you will have to do it with less exposure. It will not be easy and pictures are only the beginning. Wording of ads is vital to attract the attention of buyers. Sellers must also be careful not to violate any fair housing laws in their use of words. Phrases such as "a great family home" could be determined to be discriminating against buyers without children and are a violation of most state statutes. How to best market your home, in newspapers, social media and websites and how to place each ad is another issue that must be addressed.

If you are willing to work with a buyer's agent, you should have some sort of a lockbox on the home so you do not need to be present at each showing. If you plan to show the home yourself, be prepared to have the rest of the home's occupants off the property, including children and all pets. This means you must be available on nights and weekends, sometimes at the drop of a hat. A 2010 study by Microsoft about attention spans in the digital age found that the average adult's attention span had dropped form 12 seconds in 2000, to only 8 seconds in 2010 (Microsoft, 2015). When a potential buyer calls because they saw an ad or a sign, the ideal window to return the call is no more than 15 minutes. After that, interest in the property begins to wane. After 24 hours, the likelihood of that caller becoming the buyer drops to 22%. (Realtors, 2013) You simply cannot say to a potential buyer that you can show them your home next Tuesday or the following weekend when it is convenient for you and expect success. Selling your home has now become your full time job. On average, advertising, promoting and showing your home should take about 30 hours a week. If you do not have that kind of time to devote to the process, your likelihood of success will fall dramatically.

Once you have advertised and staged your home, and you are having showings, the next potential pitfall is known as the false compliment. Nearly every FSBO seller I talk to who has shown their home honestly believes that an offer is right around the corner. It's not that they are all eternal optimists. It is because everyone they walk through their home tells them how nice their home is. Even if it smells like cat pee and is dirty or even just not at all what the buyer is looking for or expected, most people are taught to be basically polite. So, when someone is showing you through their own home and asks what you think, most nice human beings say it is very nice and they will think about it. Then they may get in their car, look at their spouse and that is when the truth comes out. But the seller doesn't hear that. They saw a couple who seemed interested. They looked at the whole house, maybe even pointing out things that were cute or features they liked. When the seller asked if they were interested in writing an offer, the buyers said "Maybe" and said they would think about it. So the seller waits on the edge of their seats for an offer that is never coming. Most sellers are personally invested in their homes. We all become blind to some things that may stick out like a sore thumb to potential buyers. And most sellers lack training to pick up on cues, key words and questions and even nonverbal communication about the buyer's true potential interest in a home. Buyers are not lying to you out of spite. They are trying to be polite. But it can create false hope and false expectations and a seller who is riding that emotional roller coaster after each and every showing will soon find themselves exhausted.

Or perhaps despite all your efforts in advertising, you are not having many showings. This is usually a sign that your price is off, and usually pretty far off. Check your numbers again. Look at other ads. Make sure you are not making your home more than it is. As difficult as it is, you must find a way to be objective in this process for it to work. If it's not your price, it may be your pictures or advertising or because you are not on the Realtor's site, that your exposure on the market is too limited. Do you know if you are in a buyers or seller's market? Do you know the average time homes are taking to sell on the market? Do you have the information you need to successfully do this yourself?

I have heard time and time again, especially in a strong sellers' market that I am paid thousands of dollars to stick a sign in a yard, as if that is all that I do. Or after only one or two days on the market, I bring my client's multiple offers on the home and they say, "It sold so fast! You didn't even do anything! Why should I have to pay you all of this money?" If hammering in a sign were my whole job, I would have to agree that real estate brokers are highly overpaid and I would recommend selling your home yourself. Unfortunately, that doesn't scratch the surface of what I do for a living. Nor is it a fair representation of what I actually make on the sale of a home by the time I pay a buyer's agent and brokerage and MLS fees, insurance, photographers and advertising. My work for my clients begins before they ever sign a listing agreement and ends usually long after the property has closed. I look at comparable sales, neighborhood statistics, and legal descriptions. I find correct disclosures, help stage and ready the home, take high quality photographs and with them build high quality ads, and designing appropriate ad campaigns for each home specifically. I show the home, and arrange for other agents to do the same and I help negotiate offers. But that is not the end. In fact, even in a smooth transaction, it us usually only the middle. I work to ensure closing, by dealing with home inspection and appraisal issues, work to negotiate needed repairs, clear title issues, assess surveys, deal with appraisers and lenders to ensure a timely close, and assist sellers with timing of moving. At the end I pour over financial statements making sure that every penny of the seller's money is going to the correct location and in the timeliest method. I make sure that all parties, including mortgage companies and local and federal government agencies are properly notified of the sale, that, if applicable, the notices of tax liability or lack thereof from the proceeds of the sale are delivered to the correct parties in a timely manner, and educate my seller through the process so none of this comes as a surprise.

Yes, you can sell your home on your own. The benefits can be maintaining control or saving money, but the drawbacks are a significant loss of expertise, and a huge cost of lost time and freedom. Typically the mistakes that are made can be costly. From not selling your home for the price you want or need, to maybe not selling your home at all, to making costly legal errors like missing a needed state disclosure form, which can result in large civil penalties, the cost of not having a professional by your side can be detrimental. The good news is that statistically, paying a real estate broker usually pays for itself. In 2013, For Sale By Owner homes accounted for 9% of all home sales in the nation and those homes sold for on average 18% less than their competition. (Realtors, 2013) Suddenly a 5-6% commission doesn't seem so costly, does it?

    One of the biggest issues I have with people listing and advertising their own home is the money I see them leaving on the table, simply due to their inexperience. Just today I saw two ads that were detrimental to the home it was meant to try to sell. The first had loaded pictures in the wrong order, thereby making the featured picture in the ad a picture of the stairs to the basement. The next 15 shots were more of the same; basement, hallways, laundry room, all of which were unimpressive. On picture 25, I finally was able to see a charming exterior picture which showed a sprawling yard, and then a nicely updated kitchen in picture 27. Unfortunately in a day and age where the average buyer gives your home 8 seconds before deciding whether to move on, this one simple error cost that home owner potential buyers, because as the potential buyers scrolled through the internet, what they saw was the basement stairs. (Realtors, 2013) Pictures can't be random. They must be designed to provide the most impact up front. If you don't know how to organize your pictures to your maximum eight second benefit, rather than randomly uploading or even giving a room by room tour of the home, you are leaving money on the table making your home one of the homes selling for 18% less than it's professionally represented competition.

The second ad that came across my desk this morning used all the wrong words; "dead end" rather than "cul-de-sac" or "low traffic", for example. Twice they used the word "small" to characterize rooms in the home. Much of listing a home is about creating the feeling people are looking for. If the room is small, calling it something else will not change the size and telling people it is large will only disappoint them when they walk through. However choosing to call a small master bedroom "cozy" in an ad and making sure to stage the home to accentuate the large windows will add value. Saying you live on a dead end with small bedrooms is leaving money on the table, joining the unlucky homes that became worth 18% less.

While statistics are fine and good, it is hard to see how that would play out in the real world. So let me share with you only one example I have had in the last few years. It was the summer of 2015. Some friends were selling their home on their own. The wife came to me and said she hoped I wasn't bothered by them trying to sell it on their own. I told her that it didn't bother me at all. It was their home. Our friendly association didn't obligate them to use my business services in any way and didn't offend me if they chose not to. I wished them nothing but the best.

As the weeks went on, the topic would come up occasionally. I was told repeatedly how well it was going and that they were expecting an offer any day. For their sake, I hoped they were right. Then one day I got a call. "I don't want to take advantage of you, but I am really confused and I was just wondering if I could talk to you for a minute." I appreciated my friend's honesty and respect for my professional time and opinion. We talked over some issues they were having with a prospective buyer who was asking for the moon and the stars and offering very little in return. Accepting that type of offer would have left my friends vulnerable to a slew of potential problems and liability and I told her so. She thanked me and said she owed me a lunch to make up for my time, and I went back to my day. The next time we saw each other, I asked if they had it all worked out, and she looked frustrated. She said the whole thing had fallen apart. I could see the physical toll it was taking on my friend. She looked worn and stressed and I felt bad, but I supported their decision to go it alone in the big bad world of real estate. A few weeks later my phone rang again and when I answered, my friend was in tears. "I can't do this anymore!" she told me. "I need you to do it. I just can't take it!" What had apparently started as the false compliment syndrome had been aggravated by a very bad low ball, if not all together flakey, offer. The straw that broke the camel's back was ironically the one person who did not bother to be polite. A potential buyer had stepped in the door, told my friend that her house smelled and walked out. My friend was hurt and confused and overwhelmed. She was done with the FSBO process.

That night I met with her and her husband. We talked about the price they had chosen and that it was pretty close to what I would recommend, but that there were other issues with the property. We walked around the house and pointed out some small issues, that, when added together, were alarming to buyers, and how to fix them inexpensively. We made a plan to stage the home to help with its sale and I recommended that when the work was done and it was ready to show, that I would list it for 7% higher than what they had it on the market for currently. For a week, we pulled all ads and got some work done on the home. We placed some flowers and cleaned up the landscaping and staged the home. We made some needed repairs. In all, the work cost less than $1000. We took new pictures and listed the home again for $8700 more than the original price. In the first 72 hours we had two full price offers. We accepted the stronger of the two and I walked them through the disclosure, inspection and appraisal process. We negotiated some other small repairs and in 45 days, the sellers walked away with more money than they would have if they had sold it on their own, even after paying for repairs and staging and paying a real estate broker commission. But even with that, my friend told me the best part was that the weight was off her shoulders. The moment they signed the listing agreement, she said she was at peace because she didn't have to worry about it all anymore. It was my job now and I was happy to do it. I had the district privilege of not just selling a friend's home, but saving her sanity. I made them some money and I earned a commission as well. That is what they call a win win situation.

No one can say whether trying to sell your home yourself is a good or bad decision for you. For some it works out. Too often I see homes in the newspaper that have been available for too long and I know the sellers are losing money they don't have to lose. That is my frustration with For Sale By Owner homes. My job is to look after my client's best interest. If you were my client, I would want better for you.

Chapter 12
Financially Distressed Properties

There are times, even when it is no fault of the homeowner, when a home loses its value. For those who experienced the mortgage meltdown of 2007 and 2008, the fear of being upside down in your home(owing more than it is worth) became very real. Sometimes it happens because homeowners got in over their heads buying a home they really can't afford, but often it has nothing to do with the buyer and much more to do with the housing market and overall economy. Sometimes a local business closes down, causing many to lose their jobs and flood the housing market with available homes, driving prices down. Sometimes, as was the case in 2007, a long string of national economic issues came to a head and the housing bubble that had been building for several years rapidly imploded, leaving thousands owing more on their homes than they were worth.

If you find yourself upside down on your home, there are a few options available to you. . The first and best answer would be to stay put. The potential loss does not become reality until you sell. If you can, the best option is usually to ride it out.
If that is not an option, if you must relocate due to employment or financial need, this is the time to decide what course to take.

The first is a straight foreclosure. This means that you stop paying your mortgage. Some people remain in their home until the final day the sheriff removes them from their homes. Some leave earlier. Either way, the results are the same. The home is auctioned off on the courthouse steps. The foreclosure will devastate the homeowner's credit and make another purchase impossible to finance for at least 7 years.

The better option for many is a short sale. This is not a fast process, no matter what the name sounds like. It is the process of negotiating with the bank to have them accept less for the home than what you own and agreeing to write the remaining balance off as a loss, leaving you free. The process requires proof of a financial hardship, a great deal of financial disclosure and a determined amount of follow through. It is typically more cost effective for banks to pursue a short sale, but I recommend that you always have a professional short sale negotiator working with you to oversee the process. If this person is a real estate broker, they will be paid their commission by the bank at the time of closing. A short sale will reflect badly on a homeowner's credit, but would be less severe than a foreclosure, usually allowing buyers to make another home purchase in as little as 2-3 years.

Another option is called a "Deed in Lieu" of foreclosure. This is when the home owner voluntarily surrenders the deed of the home to the bank in exchange for a release for the outstanding debt. Again, this would typically be negotiated by an attorney or professional. The homeowner's credit would be damaged similar to that of a short sale.

For homeowners who want to stay in their home but are experiencing a financial hardship, they may ask the loss mitigation department of their lending institution for a loan modification. This would typically either adjust the interest rate to better reflect the current rates that you would be able to receive if a refinance were possible, but even more likely it temporarily adjusts the terms of the loan, usually making it interest only for a year or two and extending the life of the loan by the same term. This may work for people going through a temporary rough patch, but it will not improve a long term change in situation.

None of these situations are ideal, and should be avoided if possible, but we cannot always avoid the storms of life. What we can do is educate ourselves to be aware of our situations. When a home owner is placed in pre-foreclosure, their information becomes public and they often find themselves pray to the bottom feeders. Some are overly hungry real estate professionals, but much worse are those who would use your disadvantage to their own advantage.

If someone comes to you and says they will pay cash for your home and you won't owe any more money, be wary. If they guarantee that they are able to modify your loan to a certain interest rate without ever speaking to your bank, that should raise red flags. It is important to not get so overcome with panic that you let any sign of light at the end of your tunnel take you away and cause you to ignore warning signs of a potential scam. Many people found themselves victim to the worst kinds of scams and still owing money on a home they thought they were rid of. Trust in local help with a proven track record of success, which follows regulations provided by the lending institutions.

Conclusion

Real estate is constantly changing its regulations and markets, available loan products, and types of properties that are available. It keeps those of us who do this every day constantly on our toes. For all its eccentricities, of which there are many, the ability for anyone to build wealth through smart real estate investments is something that draws me to the process again and again.

The level of technology and buyer and seller knowledge has changed drastically over the years. All of this available information can be overwhelming, but I believe knowledge is power and it has made for a smarter, better educated customer. Whatever part of the process you find yourself in, buying, selling or investing, there is always an element of risk, but the reward of ownership benefits people in a way that a stocks or bonds cannot. Home ownership leads to stability of family and communities. Owning real property provides long term savings as well as a tax shelter. There is simply nothing else that performs like it.

No, it should not be your only investment in your future, but it should play a part. Do not let the ins and outs of it overwhelm you. The help you need is out there and available to you for your home and market specifically. Local is best when it comes to real estate advise. When you get advice from an expert, you get expert advice.

Bibliography

Belsky, E. S. (2013). *The Dream Lives On: The Future of Home Ownership in America.* Cambridge MA: The Joint Center for Housing Studies, Harvard University.

Buffet, W. (2009). Today show.

(2008-2011). *Current Population Survey.* Geographical Mobility.

Keeping Current Matters, CNBC, GoldPrice.org, CoreLogic. (2016). *Return on Investment 2015.* Keeping Current Matter.

Rohe, W. a. (1994). The Effect of Homeownership on Self Esteen, Percieved Control, and Life Satisfaction of Low Income People. *Journal of the American Planning Association 60 (2)* , pp. 173-184.

Sampson, R. ,. (1997). Neighborhoods and Violent Crimes. *Science 277*, pp. 918-924.

Stone, M. (2015, May 1). *Business Insider.*

US Cencus Beaureu. (2010). *Average Sales Prices of Exsisting Homes 1963-2010.* US Cencus Beaureu.

www.ingramcontent.com/pod-product-compliance
Lightning Source LLC
Chambersburg PA
CBHW052314220526
45472CB00001B/108